D1242062

MARX
and Marxism

KEY SOCIOLOGISTS
Series Editor: Peter Hamilton
The Open University

KEY SOCIOLOGISTS

Series Editor: PETER HAMILTON
The Open University, Milton Keynes

This series will present concise and readable texts covering the work, life and influence of many of the most important sociologists, and sociologically-relevant thinkers, from the birth of the discipline to the present day. Aimed primarily at the undergraduate, the books will also be useful to A-level students and others who are interested in the main ideas of sociology's major thinkers.

MARX and Marxism
PETER WORSLEY
Professor of Sociology, University of Manchester

MAX WEBER
FRANK PARKIN
Tutor in Politics and Fellow of Magdalen College, Oxford

EMILE DURKHEIM
KENNETH THOMPSON
Reader in Sociology, Faculty of Social Sciences, The Open University, Milton Keynes

TALCOTT PARSONS
PETER HAMILTON
The Open University, Milton Keynes

SIGMUND FREUD
ROBERT BOCOCK
The Open University, Milton Keynes

THE FRANKFURT SCHOOL
TOM BOTTOMORE
Professor of Sociology, University of Sussex

MARX
and Marxism

PETER WORSLEY
Professor of Sociology, University of Manchester

ELLIS HORWOOD LIMITED
Publishers · Chichester

TAVISTOCK PUBLICATIONS
London and New York

First published in 1982 by
ELLIS HORWOOD LIMITED
Market Cross House, Cooper Street
Chichester, Sussex PO19 1EB, England
and
TAVISTOCK PUBLICATION LIMITED
11 New Fetter Lane, London EC4P 4EE

Published in the USA by
TAVISTOCK PUBLICATIONS
and ELLIS HORWOOD LIMITED
in association with METHVEN INC.
733 Third Avenue, New York, NY 10017

© 1982 P. Worsley/Ellis Horwood Limited

British Library Cataloguing in Publication Data
Worsley, Peter
Marx and Marxism. — (Key sociologists series)
1. Socialism
2. Communism
I. Title   II. Series
335.4   HX56
ISBN 0-85312-348-9 (Ellis Horwood Limited — Library Edn.)
ISBN 0-85312-375-6 (Ellis Horwood Limited — Student Edn.)

Library of Congress Card No. 81-6848 AACR2

Typeset in Press Roman by Ellis Horwood Ltd.
Printed in Great Britain by R. J. Acford, Chichester.

All rights reserved. No part of this book may be reprinted or
reproduced or utilized in any form or by any electronic,
mechanical or other means, now known or hereafter invented,
including photocopying and recording, or in any information
storage or retrieval system, without permission in writing
from the publishers.

Table of Contents

PETER WORSLEY was born at Birkenhead, Cheshire in
1924. He graduated with a B.A. in Anthropology at the
University of Cambridge in 1947, and was subsequently
awarded the degree of M.A.(Econ.) by Manchester
University (1951), and his Ph.D. at the Australian National
University (1954). He has been Professor of Sociology at
the University of Manchester since 1964, and is the author
of *The Trumpet Shall Sound* (1957), *The Third World*
(1964), *Inside China* (1975), and has edited and contributed
to numerous other books, including the Penguin textbook
Introducing Sociology (1971; revised edition, 1977), and
its accompanying "readers" *Modern Sociology* and *Problems
of Modern Society*.

He was awarded the Curl Bequest Essay Prize of the Royal
Anthropological Institute in 1955, and was President of
the British Sociological Association for two terms from
1971 to 1974. He has done research, taught and lectured
in many countries.

Foreword

There are good reasons why the choice of a subject like *Marx and Marxism* for a series on *Key Sociologists* is not quite as obvious as it might appear at first sight. Karl Marx himself would certainly have said that he was not a 'sociologist', probably admitting only grudgingly to the title of 'political economist' or perhaps even 'historical materialist'. After all, he discouraged his followers from calling him a 'marxist'. Certain things he said have led many Marxists to regard sociology as no more than a 'bourgeois ideology' designed to divert intellectuals and others away from treating society as something which can be transformed through the political action of the proletariat. Yet if we choose to regard sociology as a social science whose main aims are to enlarge man's understanding of the societies, organisations and groups within which he lives — and that such knowledge also permits him if he so wishes to liberate himself from the worst effects of his social arrangements — then the impact of Marx's ideas on the subject will be seen to have been crucial. Indeed it would be impossible to understand the history of sociology without taking account of the strategic role of Marxian ideas in its formation and growth. Marx stands, symbolically, alongside Max Weber and Emile Durkheim (both of whom figure as subjects for the *Key Sociologists* series) at the intellectual crossroads which saw sociology emerge from being a vague collection of social philosophies to become a rigorous social science.

Marx developed (with some help from his colleague and friend Engels) what can best be described as a socio-economic theory of the operation of capitalistic societies, the historical factors which led to their emergence, and their likely future. It was his life's work and was intended to be the 'scientific basis' on which the working class would build the revolution which would destroy capitalism. Put very simply, the theory can be seen to have three main interlocking parts, each of them in effect *models* of how crucial elements of the capitalist system operated. One model was concerned with the 'economy' itself, conceived of as the creation and circulation of capital. A second model dealt with the social organisation of that economy, and with how it controlled the exploitation of one class by another. The third model set out the operation of the 'ideological apparatus' which is woven around the society and economy. Both the theory as a whole and the three models which it contains have moulded much of sociological thought in their original formulations as well as in the wide variety of subsequent interpretations which later Marxist thinkers have developed.

It is relatively easy to pinpoint how Marxian ideas have penetrated sociology — to identify influential books and writers, and intellectual movements like the *Frankfurt School*, for example. However sociology has not been affected by ideas alone. The impact of Marxism as a political movement in communist parties and socialist states has likewise to be taken into account. Indeed both Max Weber and Emile Durkheim could be said to have developed their own distinctive approaches at least partly in response to Marxist political movements in Germany and France, although both were well aware of Marx's 'technical' work as well. In fact it would be all but impossible to locate an element of sociological thought or research which has not been affected in some way by Marxian ideas or the hard 'social facts' of societies built on Marxist principles. Yet, despite this apparently overwhelming dependence on Marxism — either as source of concepts or theories, or as subject matter — there is in fact no single and unitary body of Marxian ideas from which sociology (or even Marxism, for that matter) can be said to draw. Rather, there exists a plethora of Marxisms each of which has contributed to the patchwork quilt of modern sociology.

Peter Worsley's *Marx and Marxism* takes this 'multiple' and open character of Marxism as its base. There can be little point in trying to present a 'pure' Marx unsullied by either later interpretations or by the varying uses to which his ideas have been put. In this way Peter Worsley is able to show both the reasons why Marx's ideas have had such a powerful effect on sociology, and the historical changes which the ideas have generated in the real world. Without grasping the multifacetted nature of Marxism, it is impossible to understand why Marx is at the same time a key figure for sociology *and* a thinker whose ideas escape the boundaries of any single discipline.

Preface and Acknowledgements

My thanks are due to Peter Hamilton, Hamza Alavi, and Teodor Shanin, who read the first draft and made valuable comments, and to Linda Ollerenshaw, Jeanne Ashton, Janice Hammond and Hilary Thorber, who typed the manuscript with great efficiency.

Thanks are due to Lawrence and Wishart Ltd. for permission to use quotations from Marx and Engels' *Selected Works*, their *Selected Correspondence*, and from Marx's *The Holy Family*; to the World Publishing Company, New York, for a quotation from E. J. Hobsbawm's *The Age of Revolution 1797–1848*; Eyre Methuen Ltd. for the translation by Steve Gooch of the poem 'In Praise of Communism'; from Bertholt Brecht's "The Mother"; and to Routledge and Kegan Paul Ltd. for an extract from Herbert Blumer's essay 'Society and Symbolic Interaction', republished in Arnold M. Rose (ed.), *Human Behaviour and Social Process*.

To Deborah and Julia,
and their generation

"Gracias a la vida, que me ha dado tanto"
— salvo socialismo

Introduction

De Omnibus Dubitandum (We ought to question everything) — Karl Marx's favourite motto.

Karl Marx has probably affected the course of twentieth century history more than any other single thinker. Because of this, his ideas have generated a vast output of writings, ranging from texts written by revolutionaries aimed at telling people how to do revolution — how to carry on Marx's work of demolishing capitalism and creating a new socialist society — to the many hundreds of volumes dedicated to proving that Marx was wrong about practically everything. As I write, in the last few months in Britain alone, for instance, Marx's theory of class and his analysis of the transition from feudalism to capitalism have been declared to be seriously in error.

Most of these attacks are written by academics. Politicians generally combat Marxism in other ways than by writing books. The growing body of literature produced by writers who identify politically with Marxism is also principally produced by academics. There is a third category: 'Marxologists', rather than Marxists: people who study Marx as they would any other thinker, whether as a case-study in the history of ideas, at times even, in an antiquarian way, without much concern for the social impact of his ideas and often without necessarily identifying themselves with Marx politically. Many Marxologists are even enemies of Marxism; for others, he is just a minor, even quaint, Victorian figure whose work mainly consisted of errors.

If this were so, it would be difficult to explain why his ideas still seem to millions of people to make very good sense of the world they live in, and show them, in Lenin's phrase, 'what is to be done' to improve it. Yet in his own lifetime, Marx's ideas had little impact. Only after his death did the first explicitly 'Marxist' mass party come into existence, in Germany. Since then, in the advanced capitalist countries, Italy and France apart, Marxism has still not 'gripped the masses' much. Where it has taken root has been in impoverished agrarian countries dominated by the industrialized powers. The Chinese Communist Party, for instance, was established in 1921, only a year after the *Communist Manifesto* was translated into Chinese, and had 57 members. Within five years, it was leading a general strike in Canton, and less than thirty years later, was in power in the country with a quarter of the world's population. The British Communist Party, on the other hand, founded in 1921, numbers around 25 000 members, and the Communist Party in the USA, according to one black joke, probably had a majority of FBI members in the McCarthy era.

Marxism has nevertheless grown as a powerful intellectual current even in the West. Despite its political impotence within advanced capitalist countries, institutionalized Marxism — communism — constitutes the major challenge to capitalism across the globe. Outside the 'West', it has taken root among the masses; in the capitalist heartlands, it is more often encountered in universities than in trade unions — again, Italy and France apart. This has profoundly affected the kinds of Marxism that have flourished in the West and outside it. Mao Tse-Tung, for instance, whatever topic he is writing on, even on philosophical matters like the dialectic, is eminently understandable, for he is always trying to communicate as simply and clearly as possible with peasants and with ordinary Party workers with minimal formal education. By contrast, the debates among theoreticians in the West are written in formidable jargon because they are not addressed to ordinary people at all, but to small coteries of other highly-educated intellectuals.

In this small book, I shall treat both kinds seriously, despite my contempt for the preciosity of the latter and the lack of interest of many of these intellectuals in what they see as the simplistic rather than simple Marxism that flourishes outside the West. Why these and other varieties emerged cannot be treated as if they were purely intellectual happenings. Rather, we have to ask sociological questions about Marxism itself by placing it in its social and political setting: asking what kinds of people took it up, what they emphasized in it, and how they used it. In the West, where a high proportion of young people go through higher education, it is the esoteric varieties that are influential. Marx explained long ago why this kind of abstract thinking should appeal so widely. German idealist philosophy, he argued, had developed in an *in*volutionary way. Since the German economy was so backward and her political development retarded, human effort was frustrated in the material world of business and politics. Instead, the pent-up energy of creative minds was channelled into pure thought: idealist philosophy.

In the West, Marxism, feeble between the Wars and under strong repression during the Cold War, has experienced a veritable renaissance in the last two decades. But although a great deal of fine research has been done by Marxists, the dominant characteristic of those who specialize in *theory* — as distinct from using Marxist theory to investigate the world — has been not just its scholasticism, but also a very rapid turnover of fashions in Marxism, including regular attempts to compensate for obvious inadequacies by borrowing from non-Marxist ('bourgeois') thinkers, notably Freud. Most of these hybrids have not been very impressive.

During the long decades when the few Marxists there were defending not only the tender seedling of Marxist thought, but also the pioneer socialist country, the USSR, Marxists tended to reject any contamination by bourgeois thought. But today, the 'Second' (communist) world contains many quite different kinds of communism, so different that they have even resorted to war against one another. The two leading varieties, indeed, Chinese and Russian, regard each other as greater enemies than capitalism. This was not so up till 1949. Until then, Stalin succeeded in keeping the new communist states in Eastern Europe and China under control. But since then, Yugoslavia, then China and Albania, broke with Moscow, and Romania became more independent in foreign policy. Still newer communist governments in countries like Vietnam and Cuba, badly in need of foreign support, as well as communist parties in capitalist countries, have been under particular pressure to choose which of the major communist countries they identified with. They have tried to resist such pressure and walk the tight-rope between the bigger rival communisms. But material dependence has forced countries like Vietnam and Cuba, in the end, to side with the communist Superpower.

Yet they still retain a fierce desire to maintain the independence which they had wrested from capitalist domination at the cost of much blood, for these were no regimes foisted onto the country by the Red Army, as had been largely the case in Eastern Europe (Yugoslavia and Poland being the main exceptions), and during protracted and bloody struggles they had developed a proud nationalism which could not be eliminated by the communist Superpower. After bitter disputes, it was finally recognized, despite Soviet resistance to the idea, that each country would inevitably develop its own variant of communism, the outcome of its unique history and of the institutions and cultural values inherited from the past. In Western Europe, it would even include the maintenance of 'bourgeois' democratic institutions, notably free competition between parties, elected government, legal opposition, and the maintenance of civil freedoms. Communism was by now a 'polycentric' phenomenon.

Under these changed circumstances, the notion that all truth could be found in a set of writings by a German intellectual written over a century ago became increasingly untenable. Those writings, I shall argue, were in any case inherently ambiguous on many crucial matters, and plain wrong on others. There had been no problem in deciding how to resolve these issues in the 1930s: Josef Stalin provided the interpretation required of loyal Marxists in the 'Short Course' on the *History of the Communist Party of the Soviet Union (Bolsheviks)* issued in 1938, after the brutal purges of all opposition, in order to consolidate his ideological control, and in the collection of his own writings, *Foundations of Leninism*, published in 1941. Unorthodox Marxists, notably Trotskyists, were denounced as really bourgeois agents in disguise, and their leader murdered.

The ideological authority, and the power to back it up, no longer exist. 'Revisionism', looking critically at what Marx had said with a view to assessing its relevance to the present-day circumstances of different countries, had been severely repressed in the Stalinist epoch, though important attempts to develop Marxist theory were made even then by people whom even Stalin had difficulty in controlling — notably György Lukács in Hungary and Antonio Gramsci in Italy. Mussolini, however, achieved what Stalin could not: he silenced Gramsci 'for twenty years'. His greatest writings were written in gaol, and were unavailable until after World War II.

After Stalin's death in 1953, revisionism could no longer be contained. Many communists now regarded the critical inspection of Marxism itself as an intellectual and political duty, not a sin. In any case, it was inevitably happening. Everyone was doing it, uncontrollably. But if Marxism had to be adapted to the historical and cultural specificities of each country, and if Marxism was not infallible, but a body of problematic propositions based on certain basic assumptions, all of which had to be interpreted critically if it was to be used effectively, this inevitably led to an examination of non-Marxist criticism of Marxism, and of what non-Marxists had contributed to the general understanding of the historical development of each society.

But the society — the *'country'* — was not the only unit of analysis. For Marx, the growth of English capitalism had in part depended upon 'primitive accumulation' abroad, the looting and exploiting of countries which soon became colonies. By the nineteenth century, Lenin showed, the entire world had become an economic and social community, as the imperialist countries divided the globe between them. The ending of formal direct political colonial rule a century later led many to expect that those countries would now 'develop' along capitalist lines. In fact, very few have done so. Why they have not is obviously primarily due to the economic stranglehold exercised by gigantic multinational corporations which — despite the political independence of the former colonies — still own the banks, mines, plantations and factories from Singapore to Peru, backed by the political force of the USA and the local capitalist classes. These processes — together with the resistance and even revolution they engendered — were clearly worldwide, not peculiar only to this country or that, and therefore generated both a sense of common interest as between Third World countries, some interest in the Second World as a market, an ally, and an alternative development model and, theoretically, called for its obverse: a general theory of what one might call 'non-development', for which purpose Marxist ideas seemed relevant.

At the same time, the post-1945 communist countries *had* developed: the whole of Eastern Europe and North Korea are now industrialized, and China is on the way. In those countries, though political freedom is restricted, no-one is starving at least, and living standards are rising slowly, whereas after 1974 the capitalist world plunged into economic crisis. Poland, a heavy importer from the West, has been affected too.

In this situation, the attractiveness of the major alternative social system, communism — now in various kinds and with its worst Stalinist aspects removed — became much greater for all but those who benefited most from capitalism. What they did admire in communism was the strength of the State machinery (including its Party system) and its consequent capacity to mobilize the masses. New regimes with strong Marxist elements in their leaderships came to power in Mozambique, Angola, Afghanistan, Zimbabwe and Nicaragua. They did so, however, with the support of very diverse classes and groups which by no means believed in socialism. In other countries, Marxists have experimented with various kinds of alliance with non-communists.

The world, then, no longer consists of one monolithic Marxism confronting one monolithic capitalism either ideologically or politically, however re-polarized it has become in military terms since the onset of the new Cold War initiated by the installation of new generations of nuclear weapons in Western Europe.

'Institutionalized' Marxism — Marxism in the form of groups, parties, movements and states seeking to promote and develop Marxist theory and Marxist politics — is now a plural phenomenon. In the world as a whole, there is no universal orthodoxy any more. Yet within each communist state, a very rigorous national orthodoxy is usually imposed, of which the North Korean adulation of Kim Il-Sung's version of Marxism is an outstanding instance. In the West, *per contra,* where communists are not in power, it is a matter of contention whose version of Marxism is the more valid. It is no longer a crime, political or intellectual, to examine what heretical Marxists had to say, nor to take seriously the counter-arguments of its opponents. It is even legitimate for Marxists to question the basic assumptions of Marxism itself. Nor are majorities or the powerful necessarily right in these debates: the Chinese ·Constitution of 1975, for instance, asserts that 'going against the tide' is a Marxist–Leninist principle (though, as in the capitalist world, this formal freedom is often difficult to exercise in practice).

To very many people in the advanced capitalist world, especially the underprivileged, Marxism is attractive as an ethical doctrine, because of its denunciation of inequality and exploitation, and its celebration of human brotherhood. Such ideals, moreover, are quite compatible with Christianity, which had until recently been implacably opposed to communism. But Marxism has never taken on as a political force in these countries precisely because of Marxist practice — the institutionalized Marxism of the communist world. To the majority of even the working classes of the West, communism *in practice* means Gulag Archipelago and 'psychiatric' wards — repression and control as the basis of everyday life, and extremes of repression for those who step out of line. Further, communist society does not seem particularly egalitarian.

And, despite the extraordinary success of transforming what was a very backward agrarian country, Tsarist Russia, into the USSR, No. 2 country in terms of political and economic might, that country has not been able to match, hitherto, the performance of modern capitalism in providing its citizens with high standards of living for the great majority, whatever the unequal distribution of wealth in the West and whatever the standard of the social services in the USSR.

That these shortcomings exist is accepted nowadays by many Marxists, who have therefore to ask new kinds of questions about what principles a socialist society should be constructed upon, and how it might be done. They are also increasingly critical of the assumption that more and more individual consumption, on capitalist lines, is necessarily a suitable goal for a socialist society or that centralized state power is the answer either.

In the face of all these gaps, errors, disasters, even crimes, which form part of the Marxist heritage, it may seem perverse that Marxism remains a doctrine of hope and liberation for increasing millions of people. In large part this is because their lives contain very little beyond daily hunger, and the experience of tear gas and torture for those who do protest. Even under conditions of greater political freedom, there seems to be no prospect of ever dislodging the rich who rule them. Further, they know little or nothing about the history of Stalin's Russia. The majority of the world's population have grown up during the quarter-century since Stalin's death, when the practice of mass terror ceased. Abroad they see the USSR as the main external factor which made it possible for such tiny countries as Cuba and Vietnam, violently assaulted by the greatest Power in human history, the USA, not only to survive, but in the end to defeat US attempts to strangle their socialism at birth, and they draw the further conclusion that a strong state is needed in their country, too. The Marxist demonstration that capitalism can be defeated has inspired parallel resistance by quite non-Marxist, even anti-Marxist, Third World countries and movements, e.g. in Iran.

To all this, the usual response of anti-Marxists is that Marxism, in the end, has succeeded — where it has succeeded — not because it is a scientific way of analysing society, but because it is a secular religion, which offers hope to people quite ignorant of and uninterested in the dialectic or the theory of the changing organic composition of capital. Undoubtedly Lenin and Mao are treated like deceased messiahs, and the revolutions created by millions of people they organized and led are often attributed to them as if they were personally able to work miracles. More practically, the gigantic power of the USSR is seen as a resource which can be drawn upon to bring about both revolution and economic development, both by governments which come to power with mass support (as in Ethiopia) and by those who have little, like Afghanistan. But the experience of revolution or the construction of socialism is more likely to show those involved that social revolutions, as distinct from military take-overs, are made not by miraculous leaders or by foreign deliverers, but by hard work and organization, and it is they who will do the hard work and make the personal sacrifices, even the dying, rather than someone else who will do it for them.

Marxism, that is, explicitly rejects the notion that our fate is determined for us by forces beyond human control, for Marxism is a humanity-centred philosophy and an activistic one. It does recognize constraints upon human action and aspiration, but these constraints are seen as principally the creations of other sets of human beings: those who monopolize power and wealth, and want to keep it that way: not as due to the will of God or to defects in human nature. Marxism, it is true, does hold out an ideal — socialism — as something attainable, despite the forces commanded by ruling classes, and often encourages people to revolution by talking of the 'inevitable' victory of socialism, much as Christians talk of the coming of the Kingdom of Christ on earth. But Christians today really don't believe that, except as a way of saying that Christians ought to live according to Christian principles in their daily lives, or that the reward for good living on this earth will come in the afterlife. What Marxists believe in is that people have to change things themselves, on this earth, where we live, and that this is the only life we have. To this extent, then, Marxism is a 'utopian' and optimistic creed. But it also insists that the success of revolution or of socialism is not something that will just happen — it has to be made to happen, to be collectively achieved, and failure is always possible. Finally, though workers may not conceptualize their experience of their working lives in terms of the theory of the changing organic composition of capital, they fully recognize speed-up when they experience it, or the loss of jobs due to technological innovation or structural breakdown under capitalism, and vigorously try to defend their wages and working conditions. They may be quite unconscious of Marxist theory, even hostile to communism, but their position in industrial society involves them in fighting the class struggle, in the words of one Marxist writer, 'every day of their lives'. Equally, though they may put up with inequality, they do not like it or regard it as just.

It is because Marx, however wrong or inconsistent he may have been about many issues, large and small, was right in his grasp of many central processes of modern capitalism; was highly critical in his mode of thinking; was able to discern the outlines of what a socialist society might look like; and constructed much of the analytical equipment needed to think all this through, that his work remains of importance as social science. In this book, I will be concerned not with Marxism, then, but with the variety of Marxisms, plural, that have been sparked off by the ideas of the 'first Marxist'. So I will not pay exclusive attention to what Marx himself said, but will also look at what later generations of Marxists have made of his ideas. It is also my belief that it has been easier for them to develop all these different versions of Marxism because Marx's own thought did not form a consistent whole either.

I propose, therefore, to distinguish between what remains valuable and valid in Marx's thought, what we may safely discard, and what is debateable — and therefore stimulating and possibly right. To treat Marxism itself in this critical way will offend only those few to whom everything Marx said is unquestionable and his thought as a whole unproblematic, and those others who think that if you look hard enough in Marx you will find the answer to everything (perhaps in some obscure corner people haven't noticed), as well as those intolerant and intolerable people who claim to know authoritatively what Marx 'really' meant and try to penalize anyone who disagrees with them (the penalties ranging from criticism and denunciation to imprisonment, torture and death): in sum, all those religious creatures to whom Marx's favourite motto is unacceptable, the kind of people he had in mind when he exasperatedly declared that he was 'no Marxist'.

To understand how Marxism developed in all its diversity, we need to start at the beginning, with its emergence.

1

The Materials
and Their Synthesis

Marx came from a bourgeois background, from a professional family in a small town. He was born in 1818, his father a lawyer in Trier, a very ancient Rhineland city and centre of the Mosel wine-growing district. Capitalist industry, the big city, and the industrial bourgeoisie, were yet to appear in Germany. Marx himself came of impeccable Jewish, indeed rabbinical descent. His father had had to convert to Christianity in order to hold public office, but was in any case no traditionalist, being deeply inspired by the ideas and ideals of the Enlightenment which had long influenced the Rhineland. The effects of the twin revolutions abroad — the economic Industrial Revolution in England and the political Revolution in France — had further affected the Rhineland long before it was more directly and brutally affected by the shock-waves emanating from France when it was invaded and annexed by Napoleon. The whole of Germany, moreover, was then reorganized by Napoleon: in 1790, there had been some 400 bits and pieces which made up the 'Holy Roman Empire'. He combined them into 16 prince-doms to form a 'Confederation of the Rhine', and after his defeat 40 states remained in Germany. The Rhineland went to Prussia. The work of political integration begun by Napoleon was thus by no means entirely undone, neither was the cultural modernization and integration symbolized by the Napoleonic legal Code, which laid the basis for a modernized society: tithes, feudal rights, church properties and guilds were removed, and civil equality (though an unrepresentative constitution), and a liberalized and expanded administrative system introduced.

But there was still no overall political entity called 'Germany', and there would not be until Marx was in his fifties. The work of integrating Germany was ultimately to be accomplished not by liberal forces imbued with the ideals of the French Revolution, but firstly and much more prosaically, through the economic unification of the German states into a custom union, the Zollverein, and finally through the military-political supremacy of Prussia, where capitalist industry was weak and the landed aristocracy strong. It was Prussia which was to use its military machine to weld all the pieces together to form a centralized state administered by a bureaucracy notorious for its impersonal efficiency in carrying out whatever the ruling class decided. The new Imperial Germany had to carve out a place for itself in a world already dominated by more advanced pioneer capitalist Powers, notably France and Britain, through industrial modernization based upon scientific innovation; through cooperation between the State and the banks to develop industry; and finally through military conquest in which Prussia successively defeated Austria and France, and in 1914 took on Britain.

In Marx's day, all this could scarcely be envisaged. Those who dreamed of German unification did not expect or hope for it either via capitalist industrialization or via militarism. Rather, they thought it would come about through the putting into practice of the ideals of the French Revolution.

The French Revolution: Social Theory and Socialist Theory

Napoleon's innovations had consisted of much more than a merely structural administrative rationalization. They had been based on the ideals of the French Revolution, though under Napoleon the more radical social changes, experiments, and movements had been brought to a halt, and what had been achieved hitherto consolidated.

The intellectual pioneers of the Enlightenment — that free-thinking movement led by people like Voltaire, Montesquieu, and Diderot, out of which the ideas that were to guide the Revolution emerged — had argued that people and societies could be and should be guided and governed by the logic of Reason, rather than according to tradition or religion. But Reason was always to be applied to the fulfilment of basic ethical ideals. Since the citizen was the basic building-block of society, all citizens should be free to pursue their interests unless they infringed upon the like freedom of others. Individual liberty, then, was not an absolute. Ideally, combinations of individuals to promote the interests of organized groups intermediate between the level of the individual and the State were wrong. Such 'sectional' interests should not be pre-eminent; rather, the common will of the whole, in the form of the majority, should rule. Conflicts of interest and minority interests were, in political theory, usually dismissed as resolvable in principle, since liberty and equality could be interpreted and converted into practical policy by people equipped not only with a scientific approach to social affairs, but also informed by a new civic ideal. Conflicts between individuals, conflicts between sectional interest groups, and even conflicts between the distinct ideals themselves, would therefore dissolve under the beneficent influence of Reason and goodwill, and the readiness to accept the majoritarian will of the people, e.g. in the form of direct plebiscites to determine what that will was.

Just as the American Declaration of Independence resoundingly begins by appealing to universal propositions: 'We hold these truths to be self-evident, that all men are created equal, that they are endowed by their Creator with certain inalienable Rights, that among these are Life, Liberty and the pursuit of happiness', so the ethical principles of the French Revolution were conceived of as absolute principles, of metaphysical status, and were treated, therefore, in a virtually religious way. Reason was actually worshipped as a 'goddess' during the French Revolution, and Comte could crown the new social science he dubbed 'sociology' with a bizarre cult of the worship of humanity. But if these were absolute values, they were thought of as deriving from a scientific view of social evolution, and not – like religious injunctions, such as the Ten Commandments – as emanating from somewhere outside humanity, i.e. from God. They were seen, rather, as rules for behaviour entailed in the social necessities of living and working together to achieve common ends. If this was religion, it was a quite secular and humanity-centred religion, and in fact only minimally used the familiar imagery of gods and cults.

If supernatural authority was no longer acceptable, traditional secular authority was equally unacceptable. Instead of monarchs ruling by divine right, the modern State, it was thought, should now express the common interests of the people as a whole. Hence radically new institutions were needed – the political 'club', forerunner of the modern political party; direct elections to General Assemblies of representatives of the people, and direct consultation of the entire people themselves through plebiscites; an Army to defend the new society made up of citizens instead of mercenaries or professional soldiers, and so on.

The purely intellectual power of scientific Reason was thus to be used in the service of ends which were derived from a new central idea: democracy. But democracy possessed three dimensions: liberty, equality and fraternity: hence rival theorists and interest groups could emphasize one dimension out of this revolutionary triad more than the others, or give them different interpretations. Today, living at a time when the real possibility that humanity may soon destroy itself is always with us, it is perhaps difficult in the West to recapture the optimistic excitement inspired by those ideas, though as recently as the time of the student revolt of the late 'sixties similar feelings enthused at least many of the young. They were powerful enough to inspire Beethoven to dedicate his 'Eroica' symphony to a Napoleon whom he thought to be a liberator, and for Wordsworth, later a quite conservative Poet Laureate, to rush off to France to join in a revolution of which he wrote:

'Bliss was it in that dawn to be alive
But to be young was very heaven!'

Amongst the innumerable factions within this vast general movement were some who emphasized the element of fraternity rather than the celebration of 'possessive individualism'. Like the Levellers and the Diggers in the English Civil War of the seventeenth century, they looked forward to a *communist* society. As long as people owned property privately, they argued, some would be rich and others poor. Equality would never be fully achieved unless people were economically equal as well as juridically (before the law) or constitutionally (as citizens). An alternative system was therefore needed in which, in place of a society where some owned the means of production and others worked for them or starved, everyone would have access to the means of subsistence, and would not only be able to support themselves and their families but would be free from the domination of moneylenders or banks and thereby be better able to cooperate with others to produce for the common good.

The communist element in the French Revolution, led by Babeuf, was violently suppressed, as the Diggers and Levellers had been. Since industrial capitalism in France was very much less developed than in Britain, France was predominantly a country of peasants, its urban producers mainly artisans and labourers. Their ideal of a just and cooperative society was therefore often limited to the model of a more egalitarian small independent workshop. It was not yet the collectivistic socialism of large-scale factories and socially-owned farms. But the communist ideal could scarcely be kept within these limits at a time when monarchs were falling like ninepins, and when peasants were finding the traditional exactions of their lords beginning to be replaced by newer kinds of exploitation, since they now either had to work for capitalist owners of large farms or, for the majority who had their own plots, in competition with these new capitalist landowners. In the cities, too, artisans had to compete with a new and very rapidly-growing form of urban capitalist enterprise, the factory.

Pioneer theorists of communism had advocated much more than the socialisation of production, however. They had envisaged the reorganization of the whole of social life, not merely the economy. They had spent much time and ingenuity inventing new 'utopian' imaginary communities, and in some cases in actually setting them up. Some envisaged new forms of the family; others its abolition. Some, like Fourier, advocated entirely new kinds of community life, where people would live in large community dwellings called 'phalansteries'. And this serious and influential socialist even went so far as to suggest not only that 'human nature' would change, but even that new species of animals would emerge: 'anti-lions', 'anti-bears', and 'anti-tigers' which would happily work hard for human beings. Everything, it seemed, was up for grabs.

The German Non-Revolution: Idealist Philosophy

Karl Marx emerged from high school imbued with the ideals of the age: 'to sacrifice oneself for humanity'. It was to remain his fundamental ideal throughout his life. Like other young middle-class intellectuals then and now, his choice of university studies was influenced both by family expectations and by the social and political climate of the time. Hence when he entered the University of Bonn in 1838, he initially embarked on legal studies. But he soon gave this up for philosophy. His studies of the law, however, which he saw as the codification of social relations, were to inform his later thinking, especially his distinction between 'base' and 'superstructure'.

Philosophy was not a rather marginal academic field of study, as it tends to be today. It was as preeminent in the Germany of the time as social theory had become in France. And the kind of philosophy that was dominant was characteristically German, i.e. idealism. The centrality of thought — of the power of ideas, or as Hegel reified it, the Idea — was the centrepiece in this conception of the world, not, as a later, more biologically influenced generation was to emphasize, because the mental equipment of human beings and the advancement of human culture depended upon the evolution of the brain; not even because of the stock of factual knowledge or technical skills which were being so strikingly added to at the time. Rather, what distinguished humanity was its capacity to conceptualize, to construct categories of thought.

Hegel had died five years before Marx began his studies in Berlin, but his ideas still dominated the thinking of the younger generation. Marx himself was, he declared, a Hegelian. In Hegel's thinking, the progress of humanity was seen in terms of the gradual refinement and 'realization' of the uniquely human capacity to understand not only the natural world of which human beings were a part, but also to understand the principles which underlay the development of both the natural world and of society. No other species possessed this ability, which made it possible for humanity to organize social life rationally.

French thinkers had developed the notion that humanity had progressed through successive stages of social development. Condorcet, for instance, in his *Sketch for an Historical Picture of the Progress of the Human Spirit* (1775) had recognized no fewer than ten 'epochs'. Societies in the contemporary world, evolutionists argued, could be classified as being at one or other of these stages; some advanced, others less so. The overall direction of evolution in general was indicated by the most advanced countries. It was an idealist evolutionism in that human progress was seen not in terms of technological or economic growth, but that these themselves were the outcome of an improvement in human mental mastery of the world, as a movement of improved and more efficacious thinking which would make possible a superior moral and social life. But it emphatically rejected any notion of a fixed 'human nature': it was preoccupied with growth, progress, and change. In Hegel's thinking, expressed at a very high level of abstraction, all phenomena were seen as processes, rather than as things with fixed qualities. Things, whether rocks, people or societies, were actually constantly coming into being, being renewed, or declining towards extinction or transformation into some other form of matter. It was only our inadequate ways of thinking that led us to 'freeze' things, as it were, like a snapshot taken at one point in time, to fix what was not really fixed at all, by a process of mental abstraction, and thereby to *make* a world full of artificially fixed things out of a world that was in reality full of things-in-process. Hegel called this reification, literally: making things.

Hegel's great predecessor, Kant, had distinguished between the world as it 'really' is and the categories we use to order and understand that world. He assumed these categories to be eternal properties of the human mind. But Hegel argued that there was no separate real world 'out there', beyond and quite apart from our mental categories. The world, rather, can *only* be known through our mental activity, and the concepts we use to make sense of the world are constantly changing: historical, not fixed categories. Knowledge was relative, not absolute.

His general conception of process and change was summed up in his notion of the dialectic. From this point of view, as Marx was to put it later, 'the only immutable thing is the abstraction of movement'. Gradual change is going on all the time, some of it repetitive. But from time to time slow, cumulative secular changes lead to more fundamental changes in the nature of the entity, watersheds as it were. These changes were not just changes of quantity or degree, but qualitative changes of *kind*. The fundamental transitions of birth and death were biological instances of such qualitative macro-changes. So were the life and death, analogically, of societies.

The model was summed up in the famous image borrowed from logic in which the *thesis* — the initial statement or positive proposition — always contains elements which give rise to radical reformulations of the proposition, and eventually to negative counter-propositions — *antitheses*. The final stage is reached when a new synthesis occurs — the 'negation of the negation' — which overcomes both thesis *and* antithesis by putting in their place a *synthesis* which is superior to and subsumes both. Applied to society, the implications of this rather abstract and abstruse philosophical image were that no society is ever free from internal conflicts, and that over time these will gradually grow and harden to the point at which a decisive change has to be made.

In studying society, then, as in the study of Nature, it was essential to separate those elements which were positive and contained potential for future growth from those which were in decline. Knowledge itself can never, therefore, be absolute, not only because new facts are always being discovered, but also because periodically we ask new kinds of questions which can only be answered by producing new kinds of facts. To take a modern instance, after Freud began writing, the facts about childhood experience and sexuality — both previously virtually ignored as unimportant or taboo subjects — assumed an importance they had never previously possessed. Thus when we change our basic assumptions, our framework of thought, a 'Gestalt-switch' occurs — a radical change in the entire way we see the world which affects, too, the way we think of the details of that world.

Knowledge was also relative in a second way: because even physically, when we look at a house, we have to look at it from some perspective, either from this side or from that: one can never see it from all sides at once. Human knowledge, then, is always relative, always knowledge from a particular point of view. (This does not mean that the house does not exist at all.)

The successive stages in the emergence and maturation of Mind — the human spirit — began with perception of the immediate situation around the thinker; then progressed to consciousness of the self; and finally, with the full flowering of Reason, permitted understanding of the world as a whole, its laws of motion, and of the place of humanity in that world.

In the dialectical movement of history, the higher forms of thought eventually won out. Since these growth elements are already present, though not yet dominant, within older forms of organization, whether of matter or of society, it might seem that Hegel's philosophy would justify what was later to be called 'uninterrupted revolution'. But the now-conservative Hegel, Professor of Philosophy at the University of Berlin and virtual official philosopher of the Prussian state, could not go that far. His intellectual daring was circumscribed by his social commitments. So he used the device which was to become standard for conservative evolutionists: evolution was declared to have already reached its highest stage — usually seen as a society now dominated by Reason, which usually meant, in reality, a society run by a class or stratum of professionals, usually like the writer: mandarins, sages, technocrats, scientists, practical social scientists, disinterested politicians, or managers working for the good of those they manage, and purporting to create and execute policy, or to advise the ultimate decision-makers as to what was good and what was not, not on the basis of 'value-judgements', but on the basis of non-partisan, purely 'objective' considerations, say, of cost-benefit, or, as we now say, calculations of the likely outcomes of different scenarios. The elite is seen as qualified for this task because it has been rationally selected by examination or via some other kind of 'meritocratic' performance believed to reflect brainpower, rather than by virtue of older and now invalid bases of traditional rule, such as birth, property qualifications, or religious authority.

In the nineteenth century, Auguste Comte in France believed in rule by an elite of this kind; in England, Coleridge advocated the virtues of a 'clerisy' of intellectuals who would act as a leaven in society — a kind of secular clergy mediating between the State and the people. In the twentieth century, variants of these ideologies are still very much alive. Davis and Moore, for instance, have argued that social class reflects the real distribution of different kinds of talent, as do theorists like Jensen or Eysenck; and Daniel Bell has argued that we have gone beyond sectional ideologies in our approach to a more scientific understanding of the world. In 1960, S. M. Lipset similarly announced that the USA was the 'good society in operation', just as, a century and a half earlier, Hegel, likewise, thought the Prussian State, guided by wise and rational beings like himself, the embodiment of Reason.

Contradiction, as an intrinsic property of everything, now ceased to be the driving-force of change, since such people, once in power, apply Reason to the running of the world. But the students who listened to Hegelian lectures in Berlin (where Marx had been sent by his father, who was dissatisfied with his son's performance at Bonn, where he had spent a lot of time drinking and writing poetry, even duelling) did not see Prussia in the same light. The 'Young Hegelians', led by people like Bruno Bauer, now developed a radical version of the master's ideas. Bauer was soon dismissed from his Berlin University post because of his radicalism, thereby terminating also Marx's hopes of becoming a university teacher, despite the doctorate he obtained in 1841.

Though they were deeply concerned with social and political issues, in their general theorizing their criticality had been fairly remote from everyday practical activity: it had been a 'critical' *philosophy*, preoccupied with the tension between orthodox religion, which installed one 'reading' of Christianity, Protestantism, as the official State religion of Prussia, despite the existence of large numbers of Catholics, and, more generally, encouraged people to look to 'other-wordly' explanations both of the causes of events and of the meaning of history and of human existence – in shorthand, to God – in opposition to the new Romantic spirit, which emphasized that humankind, not impersonal destiny or anthropomorphic gods, created human history and values, and that Nature was just Nature.

Though idealism was the dominant mode of philosophical discourse, it had never entirely monopolized philosophical debate. Materialism, which Marx studied for his PhD in the writings of the ancient philosophers, Democritus and Epicurus, had been revived during Marx's student years, and idealist philosophy in its 'new Hegelian' form had itself become quite radical: Strauss had questioned, in his *Life of Jesus,* whether the Gospels were reliable historical documents or merely myths, and Bauer had even asserted that Jesus had never existed. But a far more fundamental criticism of religion in general was developed by Feuerbach, who argued that the gods, far from creating humanity and determining its fate, were themselves idealized creations of human thought, but of erroneous human thought. Society created the idea of the supernatural, whether by attributing absolute power to a supreme Deity, or by attributing particular powers (over the rain, the seas, vegetation, etc.) to this or that 'departmental' god or other kind of spiritual being, whether personal (e.g. the ancestors in general, or particular ancestors) or impersonal spiritual forces. But these super- natural products were the outcome of mistaken thinking, an inversion of the real state of things, which was that human beings, lacking the capacity both to understand and control the world, short on scientific and technical knowledge as on understanding of society and therefore at the mercy of both natural disasters and those of human making, projected this omnipotence onto imaginary beings who were credited with being able to control the world.

These scandalous ideas attracted young radicals. Marx's circle 'all became Feuerbachians', he said. And they were soon applied way beyond the sphere of debate about religion. It was at this point that the young Marx made a further step forward, by 'socializing' the thought of materialist philosophy. Hitherto, materialists had treated the achieve- ments and the shortcomings of philosophy simply as strengths or weaknesses in *thinking*, and had concluded that the sense of human impotence which religion embodied could only be overcome by trying to convince people of the strength of philosophical materialism through logical argument. Marx, on the other hand, argued that as long as people were poor, ignorant, and therefore needful of help, religious ways of thought — however illusory — would constantly reproduce themselves.

It was in this context, in an essay of 1844 (only fully published in this century as the *Economic and Philosophical Manuscripts*), that Marx made his famous remark about religion being the opium of the people. Opium, of course, doesn't so much stupefy people (which is the common interpretation of his words) as diminish pain and give an illusory and temporary sense of wellbeing. There is more than a touch, too, of sympathetic understanding of the consolations of religion, despite Marx's contempt for religion in general, when he writes of it as the 'heart of a heartless world'. Clearly, then, religion is not merely a ruling-class invention foisted onto a passive and innocent people. It is a dialectical, two-way process: religion is needed and wanted, too.

But, even if it is an illusion, to abolish it we need much more than clear thought. We need secular social change: not just tearing down monasteries, exposing 'miracles', or criticizing the irrational beliefs that underpin them, either. To eliminate religion requires more than action oriented to specifically religious institutions, beliefs, and practices: it is the heartless world as a whole which gives rise to the need for religion that has to be changed. To abolish religion, one had to abolish an irrational and unjust society.

Contradiction was not simply a logical phenomenon — an incompatibility between propositions — but a sociological one — an incompatibility of principles of social organization out of which grew conflicts between interest groups (notably classes). (Engels later argued, in more Hegelian vein, that there were contradictions in Nature too, as when water boils and becomes qualitatively transformed into steam, but few scientists, even Marxist ones, have found this convincing.)

The revolutionary idea that Marx now developed was the notion that the source of all this inhumanity, and of the powerlessness felt by the majority, did not just lie 'all in the mind'. Rather, it lay in the individualistic nature of capitalist society, which set person against person in a competition that was basically a competition over social resources. In the capitalist jungle, the crucial resource that mattered was capital: the basic division in society was therefore that between those who had capital and those who didn't. In this way, he reinforced his general ideas about the *source* of religious ideas by demonstrating how such ideas were used to legitimize and reproduce the social order and, in particular, the 'right' of the dominant classes to rule and exploit others. It was not just an abstract 'society' that created the gods; not just capitalist competition that set human being against human being; but classes of human beings who exploited others and used religion as a social and political resource.

Orthodox religions had often preached that all men were equal in the sight of God. The idea that the poor and the persecuted, the ordinary folk who led honest lives, were God's chosen people and would enter his Kingdom while the rich would not, was also an ancient theme in Judaeo-Christianity as in most religions. But to replace the notion of a better future existence in the afterlife and the other world by the idea of a new kind of social order — a classless society — on this earth, and to identify a particular class — the proletariat — as the dialectical force that would not only overthrow capitalism, but replace it not by yet another form of class society, but by a quite new form of social organization — communism — was an extraordinary feat of intellectual and political imagination, especially if we remember what the proletariat was like at that time. Marx himself had been scornful about communism only quite recently.

What had brought him to this realization was exposure to a new environment in which socialist ideas and movements were widespread and more developed, when he was forced to leave Germany for France as a result of his political activities. Marx had turned to journalism for a living, writing for a paper, the *Rheinische Zeitung* (Rhineland Times) financed by liberal industrialists, who gave this brilliant young man (whom a contemporary could refer to as 'Rousseau, Voltaire, Holbach, Lessing, Heine and Hegel fused into one') a free hand to press for basic rights of free speech and assembly, and to criticize the Prussian censorship and orthodox religion. But the increasingly social element in his writing, particularly his defence of peasant rights to collect wood in the forests and his exposé of the crisis in the main industry of the region which was impoverishing the wine-growers of the Mosel, led to the forcible closure of the paper in 1843. He used the opportunity positively, however, for it allowed him to get married to Jenny von Westphalen, the 'girl next door', who was the daughter of a cultured aristocrat in Trier who had introduced him to the utopian socialist ideas of Saint-Simon, and to leave for Paris, where he resumed his radical studies.

In Paris, he lived at the centre of a vortex of radicals in exile from many countries, and French socialists of every variety. He also met politicized workers for the first time, and for a while even changed his life-style to a commune-style of life. Apart from the Russian anarchist Bakunin and the French socialist Proudhon, the most important person he met there was Friedrich Engels. Engels was managing a cotton-mill which his father had bought in Manchester (it still stands). He had already absorbed communist ideas from Moses Hess, while a student in Berlin, so though he led the style of life appropriate to a manager and a bourgeois gentleman in Manchester — even riding to hounds — he had become deeply shocked at the appalling conditions of the workers in Manchester, both those in factory employment and the even more wretched recent immigrants who scraped an existence from casual labour or lived on the charity of others, or simply died. He put this experience down on paper in perhaps the greatest book ever written on working-class life, *The Condition of the Working Class in England*.

Marx knew nothing of all this, at first-hand, but Engels soon introduced him to the industrial scene and to working-class political activity during a visit to England in 1845. The immediate outcome of their new friendship, however, was not a work of political economy at all, but a joint study, *The German Ideology*, analysing and exposing the philosophical ideas they had both been brought up upon. To this criticism of existing idealist and materialist philosophy, and of religion, they added a critique of a purely liberal social programme and of 'utopian' socialisms. Their own originally predominantly intellectual and philosophical critique had now given way to a revolutionary social programme. Marx had studied the French Revolution intensively, and the writings of French historians who saw history in terms of a struggle between classes. Only by revolution, he now believed, could capitalism be overthrown; only the proletariat was capable of undertaking that action. 'The brotherhood of man', he wrote, was 'no mere phrase' with French workers, 'but a fact of life'. He had by now therefore become convinced of the positive alternative to class society: the socialization of property and the running of the economy by those who produced the wealth, though in ways that were based on existing economic realities — particularly the increasingly social nature of factory production — rather than, as in the case of the earlier utopian socialists, by creating small artificial communities based on ideals of cooperation or of brotherly and sisterly love, which had earlier attracted Engels.

The German Ideology, together with the *Economic and Philosophical Manuscripts,* mark a turning point at which Marx looked back, summarized and criticized everything he had been taught in his formal education, and related it to his increasing experience of the working-class and socialist movements. He was not yet able to launch upon an extensive study of economic questions. These works, then, were very much a debate with his philosophical mentors, and above all, with Hegel.

Hegel's dialectic was now, in Marx's words, turned upside-down: no longer was it ideas or the Mind which governed the world, but social relations which conditioned the ways in which people thought. In his pithy *Theses on Feuerbach,* which he jotted down in order to sort out his own ideas about his differences with Feuerbach, he summed it up as follows:

> 'The chief defect of all previous materialism (including Feuerbach's) is that the thing, reality, is conceived of only in the form of the *object* of *contemplation,* but not as *human sensuous activity*, practice ... Hence ... the *active* side, in contradistinction materialism, was developed by idealism, but only abstractly, since, of course, idealism does not know real, sensuous activity as such ... The materialist doctrine that men were products of circumstances and upbringing, and that, therefore, changed men are products of other circumstances and changed upbringing, forgets that it is men who change circumstances . . . *revolutionizing practice.'*

This interpretation of the dialectic thus denied the notion that ideas determine social life, that knowledge is acquired simply by thinking in the abstract, and that it is an individual, not a social, activity. But it equally rejected the contemporary materialism which argued that human thought simply 'reflected' — automatically, as it were, and unambiguously — an inert world of matter outside ourselves. There *is* a material world, but we gain knowledge of it not just by thinking, but also by *doing*. Marx cited with approval Goethe's saying: 'In the beginning was the deed', and in his famous final thesis on Feuerbach declared : 'The philosophers have only *interpreted* the world, in various ways; the point, however is to *change* it'. But doing without thinking was characteristic of animal rather than human activity. The capacity to think meant that human beings did not merely react to stimuli in the form of reflexes or responses, but used their minds to interpret *how* to respond. They could also go beyond their immediate circumstances, could generalize, mentally abstract and compare experiences and ideas, could therefore invent not only new ways or new technical instruments, but also new intellectual instruments and social institutions: new ways of thinking led to new ways of doing things, and *viceversa*. We can even, therefore, imagine whole new 'worlds' — 'utopias', as Karl Mannheim was to call them — that do not as yet actually exist.

'A spider', Marx observed — anticipating the fundamental argument of modern cultural anthropology and of symbolic interactionism — 'conducts operations that resemble those of a weaver, and a bee puts to shame many an architect in the construction of her cells. But what distinguishes the worst architect from the best of bees is this, that the architect erects his structure in imagination before he erects it in reality'. Here speaks the dialectical Marx, whose sociology recognizes the centrality of mental activity, and — unlike the economistic Marx — does not reduce human activity to the material through simply omitting the 'ideal' by a sleight of hand. Rather, production itself is shown to entail both 'imagination' and the use, even in production itself, of culturally-acquired knowledge, and in turn leads to additional and novel forms of knowledge.

Human beings could also apply the critical spirit to received ideas — to 'conventional' wisdom — and not only to orthodox ideas, but to established institutions, too. To talk as if Mind were some abstracted entity with an existence of its own, unconnected with humanity, or, even more mystically, somehow 'using' human beings as vehicles of its own activity — 'materializing' itself like ectoplasm in a séance — was nonsense. It was people who thought; the brain was the organ of thought, its material source, and both the knowledge and the conceptual categories we use to acquire and organize knowledge were social products, accumulated over the history of humanity, though constantly added to and refined. The acquisition of new knowledge, dialectically, entailed a 'negative' critical scrutiny of old knowledge, and, at crucial times and points, the rejection of old facts and old categories. The thinking was done through individual brains and minds, but these were always informed by ideas and preoccupations which in turn reflected the wider preoccupations and assumptions of society as a whole, and particularly of those who dominated it.

How people thought, therefore, what they believed, and the ways in which they conceived of the world — whether the natural, the supernatural or the social worlds — were dependent upon the influences they were exposed or subjected to, i.e. their social and cultural conditioning. People did not think at random like computers without a program.

But the crucial element Marx introduced into the debate about the relationship between thought and practical activity was not just the notion that thought was a product of humanity in general — of Society or Humanity with capital letters. He also rejected the communitarian communism that appealed to those artisans who were revolutionaries because they resented the growing pressures of large-scale capitalism, but who basically looked back to a time when each could be his own master. Nor did he accept the current liberal assumption that the individual was the atom of society, its basic building-block. Rather societies were composed of classes, and though each individual was indeed unique, each individual also shared social characteristics with other people occupying similar positions in society: 'The human essence', he noted in the sixth 'thesis' on Feuerbach, 'is no abstraction inherent in each single individual. In its reality it is the ensemble of social relationships'.

There is the seed of a whole Marxist psychology, which unfortunately has never been adequately developed: a conception not only of the individual as sharing in common the social attributes of the groups and categories he or she has been part of — from the family to one's social class — but which also recognizes the distinctive individuality of every person, since the social experience of each individual is never identical for any two human beings.

By now, of all the social groups in society, it was classes that Marx saw as the most important of all. And what provided them with a crucial interest in common, overriding or underlying all others, he believed, was material interest.

Engels had drawn upon his business experience not only to describe working-class life and to denounce exploitation, but also to analyse, theoretically, why these occurred in his short *Outlines of a Critique of the Political Economy of Capitalism* (c. 1844), which Marx drew upon in his own early economic writings. His attitude at this time to religion and ethnicity reveals this new emphasis upon the economic. The belief of atheists and agnostics that people would become free once they had emancipated themselves from superstition, or the liberal belief that the struggle for and achievement of legal and constitutional rights for the individual would itself lead to an egalitarian and free society, were rejected. Important as these were, they were not enough, Marx insisted, because they left untouched the deeper source of inequality – private property. It was no use, he argued, for Jews to think they could become emancipated just by abandoning their religious identity; they – like non-Jews – would still be part of an unfree society.

Private property divided people into owners and non-owners, those who produced and those who appropriated the fruits of other people's labour. He was equally impatient with those, like Proudhon, who thought of socialism in terms of a society of small peasants and artisans, entering into contractual relations only as they wished, and with a minimal need for any monarchies or government: an anarchist dream not only based on private property and inequality, in Marx's view, but destined to be swept away by large-scale capitalist enterprise.

These new economic ideas were still expressed in the philosophical language Marx had inherited from Hegel, nor did his new preoccupation with the material mean that he had abandoned his moral critique of capitalist society. Rather, he sought to investigate the social underpinnings of that critique. This rejection he expressed by transforming the Hegelian conception of alienation. Hegel believed that by transcending the purely material, 'Man' (in the sexist language of the day) became more truly human, ever more a social creature (characterised by Mind) and even further removed from his purely animal origins and from preoccupation with basic problems of a merely material existence.

Marx inverted this. Alienation could only be ended, not – as Hegel thought – by transcending the material at the level of the mind. Rather, it was only through social cooperation, above all in production, that people could harness Nature to human ends. So far they had only done so imperfectly, and alienation would remain an intrinsic part of the human condition as long as class society persisted, for it was rooted not in the inadequacy of human intellectual powers, but in social relations. People did already cooperate in production, but the workers, whose labour turned raw materials into goods, were deprived of any satisfaction in their work because the end-product belonged to their employer. During the work-process, too, the modern division of labour increasingly meant that each person performed an increasingly specialized task, and never produced a single whole object. The social nature of work was further negated since workers were also forced into competition with each other – notably for jobs and advancement. Finally, they were at the bottom of a pyramidal authority-structure, with orders and sanctions coming from the top downwards.

If property was socially owned, and industry run by those who did the producing, these antagonisms and frustrations would disappear. Production was already an ever more social activity, but there was still the manager, the foreman, speed-up and the wages system. Once the workers took over the running of industry themselves, however, both at the national level and on the shop floor, and once private ownership and appropriation (which Marx confusingly called 'relations of *production*', when they are really relations of appropriation and distribution, or at best *conditions* of production), relationships in the workplace and rights in property, from the means of production to rights in the product of human industry, would *both* be social, and therefore rationally compatible. Hence the term 'social-ism'. The workers would now have a material as well as an intellectual interest in what was produced: they would produce more and better; incomes would improve; they would have a voice in deciding what should be produced, how it should be produced, and how income should be distributed; hence, overall, they would become increasingly concerned with the good of all, not just with individual advantage.

In the 1960s, 'alienation' became a cult-word, like Weber's 'charisma'. It was usually used as a synonym for 'discontent' or 'unhappiness'. Just as the ancient Greeks defined people who concerned themselves solely with their private affairs as 'idiots', so, to Marx, the epitome of the alienated worker under capitalism was not so much the unhappy worker as those who were happy at their work, for they were really suffering from the ultimate illusion if they could find satisfaction in such a wretched existence. More truly human, because revolutionary, was the discontent symbolized by the 'intellectual' Greek god, Prometheus, who defied Zeus and stole the sacred fire (of civilization) from Mt Olympus. Because of this, he was regarded as the 'preserver' of humanity. He was also punished by being chained to a rock, where an eagle continually devoured his (immortal) liver. Marx's strong identification with Prometheus is reflected in a famous contemporary cartoon, published after the suppression of the *Rheinische Zeitung,* which shows Marx chained to a printing-press while a (Prussian) eagle eats his liver.

Some idea of just how — to our ears — abstractly and philosophically these radical ideas were expressed can be seen from a passage of Marx's typically Hegelian prose in 1844:

'The idea of *'equal* possession' is a political-economic one and therefore still an alienated expression for the principle that the *object* as *being for man*, as the *objectified being of man,* is at the same time the *existence of man for other men,* his *human relation to other men,* the *social relation of man to man.'*

(*The Holy Family*, Chap. 4)

After *The German Ideology,* Marx became much more involved with international communism, which then was only a handful of exiles. In Brussels, where he had moved from Paris, he played a central role in knitting together the tiny group of communists in Western Europe who were in contact by correspondence, and who had already established the 'League of the Just'. By 1847, this had been replaced by the Communist League. It was this organization, of only about 300 members, which asked Marx to expound the theoretical principles of communism in a manifesto.

The *Communist Manifesto* did not get accepted without opposition. In his *The Poverty of Philosophy* (1846) Marx had already denounced, on the Right, the socialism of Proudhon based on the small producer for its ignorance of the realities of the increasingly large-scale nature of capitalist production and for its 'neutral' denunciation of strikes as anti-social. In the process, he sets out more clearly the distinctive features of his own position. On the Left, he directed his fire against the influential advocates of the conspiratorial ideas of Blanqui, who advocated the formation of small and disciplined secret societies, often terrorist ones (on lines which have remained important principles of organization for underground and guerrilla movements) and against the romantic revolutionism of Weitling, who advocated instant uprisings in which not the proletariat, but the urban poor (whom Marx scornfully called the 'lumpenproletariat', literally the 'ragamuffin' proletariat) would be let loose to vent their chaotic wrath upon the bourgeoisie and their property. Marx's contempt for this kind of ultra-radicalism did not derive from a realization that it represented the response of artisans rather than the factory proletarians proper to industrial capitalism, for he still talked of the artisan members of the Communist League as the 'proletariat'. (He was also quite ready to ignore the 'momentary opinion' of this or any other proletariat when he thought they were wrong.) But proletarian revolution was not on the immediate agenda, because the capitalist system would first have to exhaust its capacity for growth before socialism could replace it. This was not yet the case even in rapidly-expanding industrial countries like England, he believed, even less in countries like Germany where the bourgeoisie were not yet in the saddle, but where the growth of capitalism and of bourgeois republicanism were progressive developments and should be supported in opposition to the archaic landed aristocracy and the monarchical system.

It is symbolic of the contemporary insignificance of these pioneer communists that the greatest announcement of the existence of their movement, largely made up as it was of artisans and intellectuals, should pass by virtually unnoticed by real proletarians; even more ironic that one of the reasons the voices of this handful of sectaries did not get heard was that they were drowned by the crackle of rifles and the boom of artillery as the revolution they advocated really did sweep Europe. Nevertheless, the *Manifesto* did interpret the growth of capitalism in a way that was to make increasing sense to millions and present them, too, with the possibility of an alternative and better social order. It is an early statement of Marx's political philosophy, and one intended to move people into action. It therefore tends to a rather simpler analysis than that which Marx was to develop at greater length, and was expressed, naturally, in polemical and activistic tones rather than in analytical language. But it did contain all the basic ideas that Marx was to spend the rest of his life working out in detail in more thorough and careful studies written in more qualified language.

The main points of its programme, too, have remained as the fundamental transitional strategy of most subsequent revolutionary socialism. After the 'forcible overthrow of the whole extant social order', the *Manifesto* calls for:

'1. Expropriation of landed property, and the application of all land rents to public purposes; 2. A heavily progressive or graduated income tax; 3. Abolition of the right of inheritance; 4. Confiscation of the property of all émigrés and rebels; 5. Centralization of credit in the hands of the State, by means of a national bank with state capital and an exclusive monopoly; 6. Centralization of the means of communication and transport in the hands of the State; 7. Increase of national factories and means of production, cultivation of uncultivated land, and improvement of cultivated land in accordance with a general plan; 8. Universal and equal obligation to work; organization of industrial armies, especially for agriculture; 9. Agriculture and urban industry to work hand-in-hand, in such a way as, by degrees, to obliterate the distinction between town and country; 10. Public and free education for all children. Abolition of factory work for children in its present form. Education and material production to be combined.'

Naturally, Marx and Engels threw themselves into the revolutionary movement of 1848, especially in Germany. Marx shifted back to Paris at the invitation of the new liberal government, and then to Cologne, where, as editor of the *Neue Rheinische Zeitung* (New Rhineland Times), though he thought the proletarian revolution would 'immediately' follow his bourgeois one, he urged on his for once considerable readership a policy not of working-class revolution, but of the national consolidation of Germany under the leadership of the bourgeoisie, on the one hand, and of the national emancipation of Poland from Tsarist imperial rule on the other. But his policy was no narrow German or anti-Russian chauvinisms even though Marx from time to time came out with expressions of the ethnic and national prejudices he had acquired as a German bourgeois (he accepted, for instance, the Romantic notion that there were 'historical nations' and others which were not: thus the Russians and Poles were real nations, but Czechs, Slovaks, Serbs and Croats had 'no future' as nationalities, the Mexicans were 'les derniers des hommes'): it was based on support for progressive class forces favourable to the growth of capitalism (the German national bourgeoisie) against pre-capitalist reaction represented by Russia. Engels played his part in the Revolution of 1848 more directly, with muskets instead of printing-presses, acquiring military experience in four engagements that was to inform his later political writing and earn him the nickname of 'the General' amongst his friends. He not only terrified the bourgeoisie by attempting to arm the workers, but tragically met his father while directing gunners on the bridge at Elberfeld, which led to their final rupture.

But the revolutions were defeated. Marx was expelled to Paris, and came to England, where he remained for the rest of his life. There, he summed up the experience of 1848 in a detailed study of *The Class Struggles in France*, distilling out conclusions about the conditions for successful revolution, about the relationship between political struggles and class interests, about class alliances, and about the possibilities and limits of independent working-class action.

In England, he was to spend most of the next fifteen years mainly in bringing into being the first parts of his ambitious plan to produce a study of economics in six volumes: Capital, Landed Property, Wage Labour, the State, International Trade, and the World Market. The preliminary sketch for this immense project, the *Grundrisse* (Outlines or Foundations), remained unpublished for over a century, and only one volume of the first part ever appeared in Marx's lifetime, the first volume of *Capital* (1867). A second volume of *Capital* appeared in 1885, and a third in 1894, both edited by Engels from drafts by Marx, while Karl Kautsky, the theoretician of the German Social Democratic Party in the decades after Marx's death, edited three further volumes on *The Theory of Surplus Value* between 1905 and 1910. It is to Marx's fundamental and profound study of economic science that we now turn.

2

The Model of Capitalism: British Political Economy

England was to be the last country of exile for the Marx family. But they were to experience terrible deprivations there, and persisting insecurity. Apart from limited earnings from articles written for the *New York Herald Tribune* (then a radical paper), Marx had no regular source of income, but depended upon Engels, who supported him for over a decade out of his income as the wealthy representative of his family in the Manchester cotton-mill his father owned, an occupation which Engels found increasingly intolerable, but which he endured for twenty years in order to make Marx's work possible. But in non-monetary terms, as Marx noted when he sent the manuscript of *Capital* off to the printer, he too had sacrificed his health, his happiness in life and his family in the cause of humanity. It had meant years of grinding poverty, in which rustling up enough bread and potatoes for the next meal and coal for the fire, holding creditors at bay, running to the pawn-shop, illnesses of malnutrition, even eviction, were the stuff of everyday life.

Jenny, an aristocrat's daughter, soon found out what the life of a revolutionary's wife was like: having to sell her furniture; being arrested for 'vagabondage' and imprisoned with prostitutes; pawning the children's clothes and the family silver; seeing the bailiffs take the baby's cot and the girls' toys. They were unable to go to school, when their winter clothes were at the pawnshop. When the baby died, they had to borrow to pay for the coffin. Little wonder that three of their children died altogether and one was still-born, and that Marx suffered from carbuncles, boils, insomnia, influenza, ophthalmia, toothache, headache, liver troubles, and rheumatism so severe it woke him from his sleep.

As an immigrant refugee, the notorious 'Red Doctor' could not get rid of his Prussian citizenship, nor would the Home Office grant his application to become a naturalized British citizen, even after twenty-five years' residence. Marx, it is true, was not a good manager when he did have money, largely because of his bourgeois background: servants and piano lessons were necessities (just as few of his followers, though they claim not to deify him, admit that he could be quite racist in some of his more spontaneous utterances). When young, he could enjoy a night out drinking with friends, on one occasion quite riotously. But normally, he was a quite orthodox Victorian *paterfamilias*. He hugely enjoyed family life, outings on Hampstead Heath, evening poetry-readings and musical entertainments, and could even tell an unfortunate suitor for his daughter's hand that he should cool his passionate behaviour and adopt instead 'a manner that conforms with the latitude of London', whilst haughtily inquiring whether his economic position was adequate to support his daughter properly. At the end of his life, he was able to resume a style of life more in keeping with his origins, and attempt to recover his ruined health by visits to Carlsbad, Geneva, Monte Carlo and even Algiers (where he shaved off his beard).

But most of his life was a 'slavery' to politics and to his intellectual labours. The complete works of Marx and Engels run to over fifty volumes, including nine volumes of letters from one to the other. Much of *Capital* may indeed have been written in the Reading Room of the British Museum, so conducive to scholarly work, but much, too, was written on a table piled with books and papers in the single room shared by the whole family for all purposes, with the children playing 'horsey' on their father's back while he tried to write.

A small legacy in 1856, a substantial one in 1864, and a later annuity from Engels allowed some relief, and eventually permitted Marx to live more in the style of a Victorian gentleman to which he was accustomed, a style which, alas, included having an illegitimate baby by the family's maid. Engels shouldered this burden, too, by accepting legal paternity. Engels — surely one of history's most attractive personalities — was as capable of sustained and dedicated work as Marx. But he was also a romantic: he enjoyed riding to hounds, wine, a pretty face, and generally radiated gaiety. 'Take it aisy', he said, was his 'favourite motto.' He had no time for bourgeois conventional marriage and family life, and lived in succession with two Irish sisters (a relationship initially disapproved of by Mrs Marx for the good reason that she thought he was philandering with a poor girl), sharing their working-class life in the evenings as easily as he moved in business circles in the daytime. He also acquired from Lizzie Burns, the younger of the two and a militant Irish nationalist, a sympathy both for the national independence struggle in Ireland and for the Irish immigrant workers in England, who had to endure scandalous conditions of life. He admired, too, their freer life-style and the political radicalism of his Irish comrades, less accepting of capitalist discipline and Victorian respectability.

Marx, for his part, virtually withdrew from political life, after a vigorous defence of his revolutionary comrades now on trial in Germany, and now dedicated himself to the study of political economy, which was to occupy him for the next twelve years. As he grew ever more distant from his Hegelian beginnings and its tortured abstract language, he showed himself perfectly capable of expressing himself lucidly on the most complicated of topics, as shown in his short lecture to a worker's society *Value, Price and Profit* (1847), or his 1865 address to the General Council of the First International on *Wage Labour and Capital. Capital,* Volume 1, contrary to popular belief, is also very lucid and comprehensible, even in its analytical passages, and eminently readable in the historical descriptions, shot through as they are with denunciation of the exploitation of the workers and the pillage of the world outside Europe.

The basic themes had been outlined in *A Contribution to the Critique of Political Economy* in 1859. Now he developed them more systematically and at greater length. He first established the crucial differences in kind between the circulation of commodities under capitalism as distinct from earlier forms of economic organization. Under capitalism, the market was supreme, whereas in feudal Europe, for instance, only a small part of the total production ever arrived on the market for sale, not only because people consumed much of what they produced, but because they also had to hand over often more than half of it to their lord. The starting-point in the sequence of stages of exchange therefore began with the production of commodities for everyday use, most of which was immediately consumed locally either by the peasant or the lord's household and only a little of which might be exchanged in barter for other goods or to obtain money. Under capitalism, on the other hand, commodities were brought into existence precisely in order that they might be on the market and thereby make profits. The place of production and its significance in the sequence of steps in exchange had altered. Exchange-value, in Marx's terms, had displaced use-value, and capital was now dominant, the motor of the economy. But methods of production had changed, too, and were based on new relationships.

Like Adam Smith, Marx describes in detail the complex division of labour involved in the new factory-production. Smith begins his study of *The Wealth of Nations* (1776–8) with a description of the eighteen operations involved in making a pin. Marx, similarly, describes the manufacture of glass bottles. But what brought the workers, the machines and tools and the raw materials together was capital. Capital was needed to buy all three, and human labour was treated as just as much a commodity, bought and sold for the price it could command on the market — the reigning wage-rate — as, say, the wire used in making pins.

Now capital, in the form of accumulated wealth, had always existed, though when slaves worked without reward, and serfs paid rent, it had been utilized and acquired in different ways from the way capital accumulated under capitalism. The capital generated was also more likely to be used to build cathedrals, in luxurious consumption, or in military adventures than in making ever-increasing profits on the market. Capitalist enterprises, where profits were derived from selling goods produced by workers hired to do the work, had indeed existed even in ancient Rome. Merchants had also financed overseas trading expeditions to make profits on maritime voyages or overland caravans. But the main ways in which the producer had been exploited in pre-capitalist societies had not been through working for a master who paid him wages and extracted surplus value from his surplus labour. The producers had been exploited because their exploiters exercised various kinds of what Marx called 'extra-economic' control over them. You were *born* a serf, or a lord, or a free yeoman farmer in feudal society. The latter, for instance, owned small parcels of land, or had access to common lands under customary law. Land might also be purchased at times. But the vast majority only had the use of land that belonged to their feudal lords on the condition that they gave a part of their crops to him or worked on his estates for so many days of the year. Later they paid their rent in the form of money rather than in kind or in services. If they didn't, they were subject to punishment via the courts controlled by their lord as the local administrator of justice.

Under feudalism, despite these onerous obligations to the feudal lord, the small producer still retained rights in what he or she produced, and often owned some implements, however little, and some did actually own their small pieces of farm-land. But in factory production, the producer no longer owned any of the basic means of production at all: it was the textile manufacturer who owned the looms his workers tended. Conversely, unlike the feudal lord, he had no political authority over the workers. The capitalist farmer, similarly, might be a land-*owner*, but he was no longer a land*lord*. The worker, equally, was free of any obligation to serve any particular master: free to find employment with anyone, in principle, and to strike the best bargain he or she could in selling their labour. The relationship between employer and employee was solely an economic relationship: a freely-entered contract, to provide so many hours' labour in return for a stipulated wage. Apart from these economic undertakings, neither party was under any obligation to the other. Carlyle called the relationship a 'cash nexus': a contractual bond, limited to specified economic matters, and sealed through the exchange of money. Where his workforce lived and how they lived outside working hours was no responsibility of the employer; nor was the fate of those who depended upon family members who did have work. For those totally without earned income or kin, private charity or municipal relief were the only recourses.

In this kind of economy, the market was a fundamental regulating mechanism. Through competition, the less efficient firms would be eliminated, and labour, likewise, would find its price, like everything else. This theory, however, was not just a descriptive model: it was both a theory of the *ideal* and a project. 'Ideal' in two senses: firstly, in that it formulated an intellectual model of the laws governing the perfect operation of the economy, and 'ideal' in a second, ethical sense, in that the model was regarded as *desirable*: it was a model not only of how the economic system did work, but of how it should be designed and *made* to work. It was a model of how a free society ought to organize its economic relationships. The model thus entailed policy: it recommended courses of action. The general benefit of all, except those who had nothing to contribute, would be ensured because the built-in logic of the competitive market economy would lead to constant improvements in methods of production and hence in productivity. The system was therefore justified because it was efficient. Those who contributed the necessary 'factors of production' – land, capital, and labour – the theory had it, deserved reward for their contribution. The system was therefore also held to be a just one. Nor was it as 'anarchic' as its critics argued: underlying the apparent chaos of millions of individuals, each pursuing their personal self-interest, was an 'invisible hand' – the laws that governed the general functioning of the system as a whole.

Adam Smith also recognized that these millions of individuals in fact fell into three great classes: those who owned land; those who owned capital; and those who had nothing to offer on the market other than their labour-power. In Smith's model, as in all later conservative theory or in the twentieth century functionalist sociology, the classes which owned the key factors of production were seen as complementary — in feudal society, the lord needed the labour paid as rent, and the serfs needed land; under capitalism, workers needed employment, and employers, whether capitalist land-owners or industrialists, needed 'hands'. David Ricardo, another great Scottish economist, later challenged the notion that capital was the creative element, however. Rather, he argued, it was labour that was the source of all value, and which provided the dynamic without which capital would remain inert. The apparent domination of capital was an illusion, for capital itself was merely the outcome of human labour, transmuted into the form of money. It was so much labour-time locked up, 'congealed', or 'incarnated' or 'petrified' or 'crystallized', as Marx later put it, in the form of objects, whether machines, coins or banknotes. And what capital made possible, in turn, was the power further to command other people's labour, by paying them wages which gave their employer rights of ownership over the value of labour locked up in the commodities they produced.

Marx extended this notion by distinguishing between necessary labour and surplus labour. What the workers were paid, he argued, was what they needed to maintain themselves and to bring up the next generation of workers: to ensure both production and reproduction. But workers produced far more in a day's work than this; the balance, the 'surplus value', in Marx's language, went to the employer. (There has been great debate subsequently, as to whether he really meant that only those workers who produced commodities were performing 'productive' labour, which at times he appears to say. Such a view would, of course, not only separate State employees, clerical workers and those in distribution from the 'working class', but make them parasitic upon the latter — which Marx surely never meant.)

To Marx, the relationship between employer and workers, then, was by no means one of mutual advantage or of complementary 'contribution' to a joint activity. It was an asymmetrical relationship of exploitation. All workers, whatever particular factory or branch of industry they worked in, were exploited and therefore constituted a category: a social class of exploited producers. The bourgeoisie (capitalists) equally jointly constituted a class of exploiters. Between the two, there was an intrinsic opposition of interests, the employers trying to increase their profits by intensifying exploitation: working their labour-force harder, longer and more continuously; the workers resisting and pressing for improvements in wages and working conditions. This antagonism between the classes, however, was the outcome of a deeper contradiction of principles of economic organization: under capitalism the contradiction between a highly social, cooperative division of labour, on the one hand, and the private appropriation of the socially-produced goods by the owners of capital, on the other.

Marx designated this set of relationships the capitalist 'mode of production' (though in reality, it is a model of production plus appropriation). He also saw all this as the logic of a system that the people involved in did not necessarily see in the way that he was presenting it. Though the workers obviously knew that they did the hard work and the capitalists reaped the profits, they might have quite a 'false consciousness' as to why this state of affairs existed. They could not, cognitively, understand the working of the capitalist market, which seemed to be beyond human control. Sometimes they credited money with an almost magical power, like the powerful objects, the 'fetishes', which West Africans were reported to worship in the way Italian peasants prayed to statues of the saints. Money or the bank-rate were thought of as powerful *things* controlling our fate almost as if they had a personality and a will of their own. But money, Marx argued, did not talk, and these 'things', far from being independent of and superior to human beings, were in fact themselves the outcome of social relationships. It was *people* who owned capital, who ran businesses and employed workers, and it was as the outcome of competition between such people that wages and prices rose and fell. To understand all this called for the scientific understanding which political economy could provide. Otherwise, all kinds of quite false consciousness would persist: people might regard their lowly condition as justified; or accept ruling-class arguments that profits were the capitalists' 'reward' for risks they took in investing their capital, for 'giving' others employment; or they might see their own misery as some inevitable 'fact of life', as bad luck, or as punishment for sin.

Marx did not examine these aspects of false consciousness — how workers thought of the system as a whole — very much, though they are vital to an understanding of how a grossly inegalitarian class system can continue to exist and why the poor and the exploited put up with it. Rather, he concentrated on the related but distinct question of the consciousness of the workers themselves as a collectivity. For they did not necessarily concern themselves with workers in other factories or industries, even less see themselves as a class, nationwide or even international in scope. Occupying a distinctive common position in the economic system indeed meant that they were a social category, but only potentially were they a fully-formed class. In Hegelian language, they were a 'class *in* itself'; only if they became conscious of their common life-situation, their structural position in a class society, and the common interests this entailed, and only if they went on to express that consciousness by creating organizations to further their collective interests would they become a 'class *for* itself'.

Class position and class consciousness, then, did not necessarily coincide. Marx believed, however, that sooner or later, a militant class consciousness would emerge, because workers were bound to fight to defend and improve their position at work — for reforms, which in turn would be resisted. In the process they would develop better organization and extend their understanding of their position in the system as a whole. Eventually, they would arrive at a revolutionary consciousness, when class struggle over wages and conditions would be replaced by class warfare, in which the bourgeoisie would be threatened by the workers' challenge to the system as a whole, once the latter came to realize that exploitation could never be eliminated under capitalism, since it was a system founded on exploitation and new forms would constantly emerge. Only by destroying capitalism, and replacing it by another, superior economic system in which ownership and production were both social, could the central economic contradiction of capitalism be overcome and a more just and humane society created.

That the capitalist class would resist, if necessary by using force, seemed obvious to anyone with experience or knowledge of England, which had ruthlessly banned trade unions ('combinations') and deported militants to Australia; or Germany, where the popular uprising of 1848 had been brutally crushed; or, later, of France, where the working-class militants of the Commune were to be butchered in thousands or transported to the South Seas.

The horrific conditions of working-class existence, however, guaranteed the revival of the revolutionary spirit despite these repressions. Yet what advanced capitalism was to see in reality, as distinct from Marx's model, was the emergence and consolidation of several *different* kinds of class consciousness among the working class. Only amongst small minorities was it ever to be revolutionary in any political way, even if militancy over economic issues was to be common enough, at times even violent. The workers, too, were indeed to create their own institutions, as Marx had prophesied that they would — in Britain, for instance, the trade unions, the coops, and, eventually, their own political party — but these were to be reformist and defensive institutions designed to protect them under capitalism, not to overthrow it.

Because Marx's model simply denies that this is 'true' consciousness at all, it tends to discourage the paying of attention to these real-life manifestations of class consciousness and therefore impedes our understanding of working-class psychology and behaviour. And it pays even less attention to the radically differing patterns of non-economic and non-political life: the very different kinds of housing, of education, of recreation, and the differences of values and interests which distinguish working-class culture from the ways of life of the upper and middle classes. In developed capitalist societies, then, working-class consciousness does exist, but is not a unitary phenomenon: it takes various forms. But a revolutionary consciousness had rarely been widespread or lasting. Conversely, however, the internalization of upper-class ideology in the minds of workers themselves has been both recurrent and deep, e.g. among workers hostile to trade unionism or who vote for conservative parties. None of this is necessarily incompatible with Marx's model, but it does mean that the latter, in the state he left it, needs greatly extending to take account of much more than simply the presence or absence of commitment to revolution, and calls for careful sociological examination of the empirical realities of working-class life as a whole and not merely its economic aspects.

Marx's analysis of capitalism concentrated on the economy. As for the rest of the social order, he saw it as inevitable that the laws, the forms of the family, the political institutions, the belief-systems, religious or secular, had to conform to the basic requirements of the economy: that the laws would protect property above all else, and work to the advantage of the rich, and would take contract – developed to govern commercial relationships – rather than, say, custom or birth-right as the prototype of all other relationships, even of marriage; that workers' children would be educated only sufficiently to enable them to do manual jobs and to respect property and their superiors; that religion would tell the poor that their troubles were due to their own sins, and would preach rewards for good living only in another life, etc. Such connections were often pointed out by Marx, in passages of great originality and insight. To show that there were *connections* between these different areas of social life was a creative achievement. But when he came to try to formulate a theoretical statement of how they fitted together, Marx never developed his analysis of capitalist *society* with the same care and detail he had applied to the analysis of the capitalist *economy*. And in the brief passages where he tried to make general theoretical statements about the relationship between the economy and the rest of the social system, or about society in general rather than capitalist society in particular, he firstly separated out the economy from everything else, and then asserted that the economy he had thus artificially isolated 'caused' or 'determined' how the rest of the social system came into being and functioned:

> 'In the social production of their life, men enter into definite relations that are indispensable and independent of their will; relations of production that correspond to a definite stage of development of their material productive forces. The sum total of these relations of production constitutes the economic structure of society, the real foundation, on which rises a legal and political superstructure and to which correspond definite forms of social consciousness. The mode of production of material life conditions the social, political and intellectual life process in general. It is not the consciousness of men that determines their being, but, on the contrary, their being that determines their consciousness'.
>
> (Preface to *The Critique of Political Economy*, 1859)

Because this model of 'base' and 'superstructure' thus clearly has Marx's own authority, most subsequent Marxists have regarded it as the cornerstone of the Marxist edifice. Yet even in their lifetimes, Marx and Engels at times qualified both the distinction between base and superstructure, and the assumption that the latter was determined by economic forces.

Marx, at times, conveys a quite crude kind of *reductionist* materialism: 'a history of humanity as the productive forces of men' (letter to Annenkov, 28 December 1846). Engels, too, could produce equally crude, reductionist versions:

> 'The simple fact [is] that human beings must have food, drink, clothing and shelter first of all, before they can interest themselves in politics, science, art, religion and the like. This implies that the production of the immediate material means of subsistence, and consequently the degree of economic development of a given people or epoch, form the foundation upon which the state institutions, the legal conceptions, the art, and even religious ideas are built up. It implies that these latter must be explained out of the former, whereas the former have usually been explained as issuing from the latter.'
>
> (Speech at the graveside of Karl Marx, 17 March 1883)

Here, there is no *dialectic*, but a one-way determinism. Unfortunately, his followers commonly adopted this very model, which led him to have to issue disclaimer after disclaimer late in his life. The 'conception

of history' that he and Marx developed, he is saying a few years later
— a conception which he contrasts with the 'materialism' (his inverted
commas) of some younger writers — is

'only a guide to study ... The conditions of existence of
the different formations of society must be examined individually before the attempt is made to deduce from them the
political, civil-law, aesthetic, philosophic, religious, etc. views
corresponding to them'.
(Letter to C. Schmidt, 5 April 1890)

and a month later goes even further:

'According to the materialist conception of history, the
ultimately determining element in history is the production
and reproduction of real life. More than this neither Marx
nor I have ever asserted.'
(Letter to J. Bloch, 21 September 1890)

Unfortunately, they *had* asserted more than that. By now, it was even
becoming quite unclear as to what *was* being asserted:

'... If someone twists this into saying that the economic
element is the *only* determining one, he transforms that
proposition into a meaningless senseless phrase. The economic
situation is the basis, but the various elements of the superstructure — political forms of the class struggle and its results,
to wit: constitutions established by the victorious class after a
successful battle, etc. juridical forms, and even the reflexes of
these actual struggles in the brains of the participants, political
juristic, philosophical theories, religious views and their
further development into systems of dogma — also exercise
their influence upon the course of the historical struggles and
in many cases preponderate in determining their *form*. There
is an interaction of all these elements in which, amid all the
endless host of accidents ..., the economic movement finally
asserts itself as necessary ....

There are thus innumerable interesting forces ... which
give rise to one resultant — the historical event ... the product
of a power which works as a whole *unconsciously* and without
volition. For what each individual wills is obstructed by
everybody else, and what emerges is something that no-one
willed ... The wills of individuals — each of whom desires
what he is impelled to by his physical constitution and exter-

nal, in the last resort, economic, circumstances ... – do not attain what they want but are merged into an aggregate mean, a common resultant, [but] it must not be concluded that they are equal to zero ...

Marx and I are ourselves partly to blame for the fact that the younger people sometimes lay more stress on the economic side than is due to it. We had to emphasize the main principles *vis-à-vis* our adversaries, who denied it, and we had not always the time, the place or the opportunity to give their due to other elements involved in the interaction.'

(*ibid.*)

He swerves, *en passant,* into a probabilistic theory of determination ('something that no-one willed'), but what *does* ultimately determine history is still 'the economic', even if only 'in the last resort'. 'The most amazing rubbish', he says, had been produced by 'Marxists' who interpreted 'materialism' as meaning 'economic determinism'. But because he adheres to the model of the economic abstracted as the 'base', and of a 'non-economic' superstructure, and by further asserting the *crucial* priority of the economic – *however* much it is qualified by words and phrases like 'ultimately', 'in the last resort', 'finally' etc. – his sociology remains an economic determinism, not a dialectical sociology. By now Engels is confused and confusing as to whether the economic *determines* the rest, or whether there is simply an *interaction* between the economic and the non-economic. (Marx himself had used words like 'conditions', 'determines', 'corresponds', etc. very loosely, and therefore ambiguously.) Ideas, Engels tells Schmidt a month later, in a letter, 'react back' on the economic sphere 'because they influence the distribution of property' (letter of 27 October 1890). By 1893, he is telling Mehring that the

'*derivation* of political, juridical and other ideological notions ... from basic economic facts [neglects] the formal side – the ways and means by which these notions, etc. come about ...'.

(Letter of 14 July 1893)

'All action', he acknowledges, 'is *mediated* by thought'; ideology is 'a process accomplished by the ... thinker, self-consciously'. But ideology is '*false* consciousness. The real motive forces impelling him remain unknown to him'.

A final important qualification to crude economic determination is his insistence on the cultural legacy of the past, including modes of thought:

> 'in every sphere of science, material which has formed itself independently out of the thoughts of previous generations and has gone through its own independent course of developments in the brains of these successive generations.'

It is 'fatuous', he says, to deny that ideas have any 'effect upon history'. By now, he has even admitted not only a high degree of autonomy for ideas, but that they are produced *as ideas* ('in brains'), and persist from one generation to another. Engels is on the brink of a theory of culture. But he never made it. Instead, he falls back on the notion of thought as superstructure determined — though commonly we are unaware of it — by 'ultimately' economic forces. A science of knowledge, then, becomes reduced to the knowledge of economics.

To some subsequent 'hard-line' Marxists, these qualifications by Engels are senile ramblings and political concessions to his bourgeois opponents; to others, evidence of maturity and of an incipient, more truly dialectical sociology.

In their empirical researches, both Marx and Engels sometimes departed altogether from the base/superstructure model. In writing about other social formations than capitalism, Marx noted that under feudalism, for instance, it had been political institutions, not economic, which were the decisive source of power in society. It was by virtue of command over military and civil power, not because they controlled capital, that the nobility became a ruling class, and thereby acquired ownership of the land and domination over their serfs, and were able to maintain their economic privileges. But in other kinds of society, in those with hunting-and-gathering economies, for example, there was no private property in the means of production (spears, boomerangs, bows and arrows, wild animals and naturally-occurring vegetables and fruits being available to all). Hence, there were not even economic classes, and the most important social bonds were neither economic, nor political, but ties of kinship.

Obviously, the relationship between economic and other institutions varied in different kinds of society. There was no absolute model valid for all societies. Yet later Marxists have commonly treated the model Marx developed for capitalism as if it were universally the case that economic relationships were always primary; anyone who questioned this belief was denounced as a 'traitor' to Marxism and socialism. Only recently has the validity of the model been seriously challenged by Marxists themselves, not surprisingly by anthropologists who have studied societies where forms of the family and of kinship are clearly not merely consequences of the need to work and produce with others, but themselves determine not only which others — one's kin — one works with, but also whom one may or may not marry, who one worships with, lives with and so on, and the way these activities should be conducted. Yet contemporary Marxists, like Engels before them, also continue trying to reconcile these findings with the base/superstructure model by various intellectual and verbal contortions and jesuitical casuistries: arguing that kinship or religion may be the actually 'dominant' but that economics is still 'determinant' or more 'fundamental' or, like Engels, argue that the economy determines 'in the end' — though they never prove these assertions or show us how they can define 'the end' (which never seems to come in tribal societies); or that kinship or religion are actually 'economic' in their 'function' — they are 'conditions' or 'instances' of economic activity since the lineage or the Church may control or affect production-relations. What they never admit is that kinship is kinship, and cannot be understood only in terms of its (undoubted) economic aspects, since these are only one dimension of kinship, which covers a range of relationships much wider in scope than the economy alone.

— It seems simpler and more scientific to conclude that Marx and Engels were right in insisting that it is necessary for people to produce, that social life cannot be sustained unless production is organized, and that both production and exchange entail crucial patterns of relationships. Other institutions, too, do have to be compatible with the economy. But the 'fit' can be quite loose; cultural forms, from art-forms to forms of religion or family codes, can persist and be made compatible with quite different 'modes of production', and need only be slightly altered in the process, not totally reconstituted or replaced. Nor does capitalism *cause* Protestantism, or need it in order to continue in being.

Marx and Engels mercilessly exposed the hypocrisy and mystification practised by exploiting classes who dress up and disguise their interest in keeping society unequal by rhetoric about 'civil' equality, equality in the sight of God, and so forth, or the 'common' interests and status of all members of society as citizens or believers. They also admitted that they had sometimes over-emphasized the economic and the material in opposition to the dominant idealism of their day, with its windy talk of 'the Idea' or 'the Mind' as if ideas were a force outside humanity altogether, dominating social life. In rejecting idealism, as Weber rightly observed, despite their protestations, they tended to replace it, more often than not, by an 'equally one-sided' materialist economics rather than by a dialectical social science in which ideas influenced behaviour, and *viceversa*. Economic behaviour has to be seen as informed by social values, and the economy as influenced by non-economic relations. It is significant that Marx's greatest intellectual achievement is *Capital*, a study in political economy, and that he never produced any parallel study of non-economic institutions, or a systematic *sociology* of society (or even of any particular society) as a whole. Inevitably, the crude, one-way model of base and superstructure actually proves inadequate even for analysing capitalism, and, oddly enough, shares with the 'bourgeois' classical *laissez-faire* theorists of whom Marx was so scornful the central assumption that the economy is somehow separate from the rest of society and plays the key role in shaping society as a whole. They, too, emphasized the 'cash nexus' as the key relationship in capitalist society, upon which all other relationships, such as the rights and duties embodied in the marriage contract, were modelled.

The more radical of them could even, like Marx, denounce the way people were dehumanized by being treated as things – their labour-power bought and sold as commodities on the market; reduced to the status of 'hands', rather than persons with many other facets to their social and individual identities; starved and brutalized. To understand why this abuse of their humanity did not result, however, in endemic revolt and total non—cooperation (a problem even more sharply posed in the case of slave society, where slaves were literally regarded simply as instruments of labour which happened to have the power of speech), requires the introduction into the analysis of elements which are not economic at all and which bourgeois classical economists did not attempt to work out, since, having separated out 'the economic', they regarded the rest of society as something to be studied by other kinds of social scientists.

Marx, like his bourgeois adversaries, also consciously concentrated primarily on the economy. In so doing, he pushed into the background everything that was not strictly economic. This is a perfectly valid scientific procedure as a starting-point: relations of production and exchange can and should be studied systematically, but we cannot stop there and simply leave unexamined the relative importance of the non-economic or *assume* – but not *prove* – that the non-economic is subsidiary without actually examining how non-economic institutions come into being and are sustained, and just how the political institutions, for instance, affect the economy. Basically, Marx, like his bourgeois predecessors, despite his frequent and genuine claims to be occupied with developing a science of society, and not just an 'economics', too often wrote as if the economy somehow operated 'in itself', as if the 'law of motion of modern society' was an economic law, and as if we could conceive of 'purely economic' relations independently of and determining everything else — the polity, the family, the dominant belief system, etc. — expressed in the unsatisfactory model of society as divided into 'base' and 'superstructure'. In his theoretical pronouncements, he frequently explicitly denies a one-way causal relationship, but when he does treat of the non-economic, it is usually to demonstrate that such institutions could be shown to be affected by material considerations. Even quite abstract concepts could be said to have had their origins in economic relationships: the German words for 'general' and 'particular', he argued, derived from different forms of landownership in ancient times.

This connecting of ideas, concepts and values to their economic origins or functions is often both true and enlightening. But ideas can be and are developed independently of any economic utility they might possibly possess. Whether inventions, for instance, get put to productive use may well depend on whether they are profitable. Innovation may even be repressed if it challenges the political dominance of the dominant classes, as in the case of manufacturing industry in imperial China. But new science, new attitudes to work or to profits, can arise quite independently of the way existing production is organized, and indeed causes changes in productive methods and relations themselves.

Much of this one-sided causality has been blamed onto Engels, who is accused of transforming Marx's 'dialectical' thinking into a 'positivistic' theory based on the natural sciences, where the subject-matter does not involve human purposes or beliefs, or cultural innovation and growth — since clouds do not think, trees feel envy, or amoebae invent things. But Marx himself constantly writes in the same 'positivistic' and even reductionist way: in one passage arguing that 'the hand-mill gives you society with a feudal lord; the steam-mill, society with the industrial capitalist', and elsewhere that in 'large-scale industry . . . revolution begins with the instruments of labour'. But in asserting that 'the various economic epochs are distinguished from one another, not by differences in what is made, so much as by differences in the instruments of labour', he does not usually mean economy and society are determined by technological factors. Technological innovation, and production relations, are themselves only part of wider systems of ownership and exploitation. But though Marx, like his bourgeois predecessors, still called his studies 'political economy' (meaning what we today would call the 'social sciences'), and did not, *in principle*, erect rigid boundaries between what later became 'economics' or 'political science' (and even later a whole host of other, newer 'social sciences', notably psychology and sociology), in his actual analyses he usually treated production and exchange with very little systematic theoretical reference to non-economic relationships, and also failed to theoretically establish the nature of the relationships between the economic and the non-economic. In Marx, the traffic was all too often presented as one-way: the economic determined the non-economic. It was a political economy that stopped short of becoming a sociology: a science of *society* in all its aspects.

This can be seen most basically in Marx's treatment of the concept of the mode of production itself. Production, he argued, requires the use of tools or instruments (from hoes to lathes) upon objects (the soil, iron ore, etc.); together, objects and tools may be said to constitute the *means* of production. But even the simplest of economies is built around some division of labour: different tasks which some specialize in and others do not. Who does what, and how work tasks are coordinated and controlled, constitute the *relations* of production. Where one class own the basic means of production, they can also control the division of labour in the production process. In the capitalist factory, the structure of authority and status in the workplace is in the hands of 'management'. These relations are, however, two-sided. They *contradictorily* involve both cooperation and exploitation. Marx used the term 'relations of production' rather generally to refer both to authority exercised in the workplace and to the private appropriation of the product outside it, because exploitation takes place both at or during production as well as after the finished commodity enters the circuit of exchange by being put on the market.

But if we look at production (the 'labour process' in modern Marxist terminology) itself, we see that production is not simply an 'objective' process, but contains crucial elements which are not material at all, but ideal. Ideal, firstly, because 'know-how' involves skills: *knowledge* of how to do a job, learned and carried round in the head; ideal in the second, normative sense, in that working together involves behaving according to certain socially-acquired and socially-accepted norms and values: concepts of duty, responsibility, of 'reasonable' levels of output (such as a 'fair day's work'), which, above all, involve an acceptance of the (often unquestioned) right of owners of property and capital to appropriate the product, or the equally amazing acceptance of their right to close factories in which thousands may work, sell the plant, or through inheritance, to hand it on to another generation which has done nothing to earn it.

When 1% of the population own a third of the wealth of society, as is normal in capitalist society, the question as to why the (poor) majority accept this state of affairs has to be answered. Some Marxists argue that there's not much people can do about changing it, but most accept that it is scarcely possible to explain acceptance of such massive inequalities without giving some weight at least to *ideas* about *rights* to property, and the *duty* to work and fulfil *obligations* to the employer, and that production arrangements themselves depend upon the operation of internalized values and norms. Though he sometimes spoke of both 'subjective' and 'objective' components in the mode of production, Marx, like most later Marxists, more often wrote of all this as a purely 'material' base, which it is not.

At times, he recognized this: force was 'itself an economic power', and the revolutionary class the 'greatest productive power', out 'of all the instruments of production'; even theory became a 'material force' once it had 'gripped the masses' — compressed and cryptic formulations which fail to distinguish between economic relationships proper and *non-economic* phenomena which have *material consequences* (e.g. affect economic relations), by using a sleight-of-hand which defines them *as* 'material' — which they are not.

For all his principled and profound hostility to bourgeois economists, then, Marx generally shared with them the purely capitalist conception of the 'economy-in-itself', with a wall around it, as it were. At the level of institutions, too, he shared with them the notion that the market is the decisive causal mechanism and that the rest of the social order is either subsidiary in significance or determined by the economy. There are many points in his more empirical work in which he does not interpret social life in this way, or does not isolate the economy and give it causal priority, and he frequently claims to be developing 'political economy' or uses the quite different eighteenth-century model in which 'society' is not decomposed into the economy and the rest, but into 'State' and 'civil society' — the latter *including* the economy.

But the conception of 'civil society' as something separate from the State was not to be further developed until it was taken up by Gramsci in the next century. Other Marxists, such as Althusser, tried to obliterate the distinction by treating institutions such as the family, the law, etc. simply as parts of the system of state control.

In volume one of *Capital*, in some of the most incisive pages ever written, Marx describes how the weight of the entire range of social institutions was brought to bear upon the working class in order to prepare them for their new role in economy and society: to turn them into reliable workers and citizens, and to keep them and their children that way. The working class, that is, did not become what they became simply because work-relations in themselves brought about their total transformation as human beings. Rather, though they certainly developed their own vigorous and varied working-class values and class cultures, their place in production itself grew out of a transformation of other institutions, and the new economic relations depended upon inducing the working class to accept their place in a system which overwhelmingly benefitted others, not them. According to the *laissez-faire* theory dominant at the time of the Industrial Revolution, the State ought only to intervene in social life to protect property, to defend society against external attack, and to regulate disputes between citizens. This myth of the so-called 'night-watchman state', however, scarcely applied to the British governments which drove hundreds of thousands off the land through parliamentary Enclosure Acts, forced them into the slums of the new industrial cities, and repressed both rural and urban resistance by vicious legislation and governmental terror, and deployed similar violence in creating colonies.

But governments did not rely solely upon force. Machiavelli, centuries earlier, had counselled the wise prince to use force where necessary. But persuasion, including 'fraud', was perfectly adequate much of the time. So governments ought to try to get those they ruled to acquiesce: in Weber's terminology, to persuade the citizenry of the *legitimacy* of their rule, and thereby convert mere rule by force (power) into rule by consent (authority). Partly in response to increasingly violent mass political resistance both in the countryside and in the cities, and because other ways in which the community had coped with poverty, via the Poor Law, no longer applied in the growing cities, the more far-seeing masters began to introduce rudimentary 'welfare': at work, nothing much more, in the first instance, than limiting excessive hours of labour and introducing minimal safety regulations; outside work, the provision of 'elementary' schools where workers' children could learn the three R's and to accept their situation in life. The ruling class also launched a religious offensive to countervail the new nonconformist movements among the working class and — far worse — paganism and atheism. Ambitious leaders could also be bought off. These new 'reliable' elements among the skilled, better-paid working class could eventually even be trusted with the vote — 'incorporated' into the political system.

The new working class was thus 'made' to accept a role for itself within capitalism — not without the vicious use of force at critical points and junctures and not without sustained resistance. Engels himself noted, in the late 1840s, that improved housing was beginning to be provided. But the basic emphasis in what he and Marx were writing was still upon the inevitability of the polarization of society into 'two great opposing camps', the bourgeoisie and the proletariat, in which the intermediate classes (notably the numerous small traders and masters who constituted, then, the 'petty' bourgeoisie) would be forced by competition down into the ranks of the proletariat (and a few ascending into the ranks of the bourgeoisie). Only in the last years of their lives did Marx and Engels recognize — and then in private correspondence rather than by amending the 'polarization' model — that the English working class themselves were become 'bourgeoisi-fied":

> 'The English proletariat is actually becoming more and more bourgeois, so that this most bourgeois of nations is apparently aiming ultimately at the possession of a bourgeois aristocracy and a bourgeois proletariat *as well as* a bourgeoisie'.
>
> (Letter to Engels, 7 October 1858)

Indeed, they went too far, for though their comments might have been valid for a small 'labour aristocracy', they were not for the vast numbers of unskilled workers like the gas-workers and the dockers who were just beginning to develop new militant mass trade unions. The eventual formation of a reformist 'social democratic' independent working-class party, in 1901, showed that Labour had finally emerged politically, too, but, despite the presence of important socialist militants in the leadership, as a quite *non*-revolutionary force.

As acute observers, Marx and Engels grasped the significance of these changes in practice, but this did not lead them to ask whether their earlier theoretical assumptions about the inevitability of class war and of proletarian revolution needed rethinking. Both were simi-larly acutely aware of how ethnic divisions among the working class — especially English prejudice against the Irish — were used to divide the working class.

On a wider canvas, Marx saw that the extension of the power of capitalist countries over the whole world was only the logical outcome of the process he had explained long ago in the first volume of *Capital*. Modern capitalist production, he had shown, increasingly took place in even larger factories, with an increasingly complex and detailed division and mechanization of labour. Since, in his view, value was only created by labour, capitalism had a built-in tendency to increase that part of capital represented by machines ('constant' capital) at the expense of reducing the number of workers in employment ('variable' capital).

This he called the 'law' of the 'changing organic composition of capital'. Since the workers thus displaced (the unemployed and impoverished) would no longer be able to buy the increasing volume of goods produced, over-production and under-consumption would cause periodic crises — slumps and mass unemployment — followed by periods of recuperation and expansion, but always tending towards increases in the scale and severity of crisis that eventually would cause the breakdown of the whole system. Not only workers, but the petty bourgeoisie and even large firms would suffer too, because, as less labour was used, the level of profits would decline, and the weakest firms would go to the wall. The increasingly organized working class would eventually be able to take advantage of this progressive malfunctioning to mobilize decisive support to seize power and introduce socialism.

The history of advanced capitalism has indeed included endemic poverty and cycles of boom and slump. But it has also seen the steady intervention of the State in the attempt to control these oscillations, firstly, by resisting, of course, any management of the crisis at the expense of the rich, but by also regulating the operation of the market (through tariffs, price supports, control of the money supply, etc.) and eventually even the taking-over of whole sectors of industry ('nationalization'); and secondly, by the introduction of 'welfare' measures to provide minimal insurance against unemployment, sickness and other disasters. This kind of political intervention by the State is not explicable in terms of the simple model of the economy as determining the nature of the rest of the social system.

Capitalist enterprise had also, from its beginnings, ranged far beyond the boundaries of the 'home' country. Though the bulk of capital had been generated at home in agriculture and industry, gigantic profits accumulated through overseas trade, in which military force and State assistance had been crucial ingredients, had also helped finance the Industrial Revolution in Europe. But that revolution itself had only been possible because a political revolution had occurred over a century earlier, which had left the rising bourgeoisie with power over the State, which it then used to engender the capitalist transformation of agriculture and industry. The process, then, was not a one-way traffic from the economic to the political, or the seizure of State power by a mature bourgeoisie. It was a dialectical interplay between polity and economy. The bourgeoisie, though powerful and growing, was predominantly only a merchant class, not an industrial bourgeoisie engaged in 'machinofacture', and was unable, therefore, to definitively conquer and eliminate the older ruling class which still dominated the crucial economic sector of agriculture. Instead, they fused with the landowning aristocracy, by using capital owned by that class to invest in industry, to modernize agriculture along capitalist lines, and to develop mines on the estates of the great nobles. Socially, they literally interbred, as the new bourgeoisie married into the ranks of the aristocracy or got themselves ennobled.

By Marx's time, Britain was dependent for much of its raw materials in industry on imports from colonial territories, and her manufactures were sold the world over. The scale of operations of capitalism was thus increasingly socialized, because it involved the bringing together of materials from all over the world and because, internally, too, production increasingly took place within enterprises that employed thousands of workers.

Marx showed how capital was being concentrated and centralized in an ever-diminishing number of really great giant firms, a process which could only culminate in the monopoly of entire branches of production by single firms, which were increasingly 'social', too, in their financial and managerial structures, since the vast quantities of finance involved now had to draw upon the savings of a wide spectrum of small investors rather than a few magnates, and eventually resulted in the joint-stock company, with limited liability for its shareholders. Managerially, the large corporation was now run, not by working owners, but by a new stratum of managers. Marx noted the emergence of the joint-stock company and the divorce of ownership from management, but concluded rather that private ownership was therefore an anomaly, contradicting the new, social form of production growing up within capitalism.

Since his time, theorists like James Burnham in the 1930s have argued that given the sometimes hundreds of thousands of shareholders of shares in big corporations like General Motors or ICI, ownership is now so widely diffused that 'no-one' owns the company, or — as an exhibition I once saw on Wall Street put it — capitalism has become 'people's capitalism'. It is the managers who really run the corporation, and their primary aim is to ensure the survival and growth of the enterprise in a competitive world, to the benefit not only of its share-holders, but also of its many thousands of workers. This breed of 'socially responsible' manager, it is argued, is not primarily concerned with the maximization of *profits* at all. As they do not own the firm, they are more likely to declare lower dividends on shares and to plough back more into future expansion. Such corporations, then, are not really 'capitalist' in the traditional sense at all.

Critics of this thesis observe that the firms still have to make capitalist profits, and exploit their workers to do so; that directors are normally recruited from the top social class and very often, in addition to their salaries, have financial interests in the corporations they work for. They commonly own large blocks of shares themselves, and their valuable 'perks', as well as the 'deferred' income such as the 'golden handshakes' taken on retirement, commonly take the form of stocks and shares in the company. All this, and their promotion prospects, depend upon the continual prosperity of the corporation and upon their contribution to its sustained growth. Further, the giant corporations *are* owned — by the handful of holders of big blocks of shares (often 'institutional' shareholders, mainly banks, insurance corporations and holding companies) which can effectively outvote the myriad of tiny passive shareholders. Only in funny Hollywood movies, like *The Solid Gold Cadillac,* do the small shareholders ever get to have a say. And the workers, even where 'joint consultation' procedures exist, generally only influence 'welfare' issues. They play no part in production and development decisions, and plants may even be sold or closed whether they like it or not. Only via their trade unions can they attempt to influence management, though normally this pressure is limited to issues of employment conditions.

The 'managerialist' critique of Marx has therefore not been very damaging, because private ownership still remains the basis of decision-making power. More serious are those criticisms which point to changes, not in the capitalist firm, but in the working class, for the composition of the working class has undergone numerous changes since Marx's day. By 1940, there were already more non-manual workers in the USA than manual, a watershed only passed in Britain after the Second World War. This growing segment of the working class, it is argued, being better paid and of higher social status, increasingly tends to see itself as *middle*, not working class. The generally accepted conclusions of research, however, show that income differences between manual and non-manual workers have narrowed. Clerical workers are not that much better off, and although their status and working conditions are generally still superior to those of non-manual workers, even the most prosperous among them do not identify as a bloc with the middle classes. Nor do the better-paid manual workers cease thinking of themselves as working class or lose their working-class attachments by adopting a middle-class style of life. Most workers, too, manual or non-manual, retain a critical attitude to the privileges enjoyed by the rich.

In political terms, the new non-manual service sector is very divided, in the UK, for instance, as between Conservative and Labour, though a sizeable proportion of manual workers also vote Conservative. In the USA, the working class has not even produced a party of Labour to this day. But the new working class has proved to be as economically class conscious as their manual predecessors. They have flocked into trade unions, and many of the biggest and most militant unions are unions of non-manual, even professional, workers, especially the ever-growing army of public employees (the health industry, it has been claimed, is the biggest employer of labour), who tend to display a particular militancy *vis-à-vis* governments, since it is the latter who employ them and who directly control the salaries they get, often for political motives, such as to keep wage demands in the private sector down by awarding low rises in the public sector, or conversely giving privileges such as inflation-proofed pensions to civil servants who are both well-organized and able to threaten the day-to-day functioning of government.

The working class is thus divided into distinct sub-strata horizontally. But it is also further divided insofar as the lowest-paid occupations are disproportionately recruited from categories of labour marked off and stigmatized by virtue of their ethnic identity: in Western Europe, by eleven million immigrants from the poorer Mediterranean countries; in England from the Indian sub-continent and the Caribbean, and in the USA by twenty-five million 'Hispanics' from Mexico, Puerto Rica and Cuba. This division within the working class has been described as a 'dual labour market' in which those thus ethnically discriminated against constitute an 'underclass'.

The largest underpriviliged minority of all are women, who are doubly discriminated against and exploited, economically and non-economically. Economically, though they are divided by class — there being rich and professional as well as poor and immigrants among women — they are disproportionately over-represented among low-earners. On average, in the UK, where half of all married women work outside the home and one in six are the chief supporters of their families, they receive about two-thirds of the male wage. But women also do much more work *inside* the home than men, managing a home and coping with the care of the children, unpaid, since their domestic labours are not rated by society as 'work'. Outside work and the home, all women are further subject to sexist treatment in every area of life.

Marx's analysis of class emphasized horizontal differentiation along economic lines. This remains valid. The composition of the working class has certainly changed, then, as Marx believed it would, though not in the *way* he prophesied; that the central change would be in the direction of greater class consciousness. In one sense, this *has* happened: class consciousness in economic terms and in terms of felt and resented status differences are indeed widespread. But in the sense he had in mind — in a class consciousness which would necessarily be a revolutionary political consciousness — this has not been the case in the advanced capitalist countries.

Marx paid little attention, however, to the non-economic bases of differentiation between classes and within them, and in his theoretical model systematically ignored exploitation based on gender or ethnicity rather than on differential relationship to the means of production: on private ownership and wage-labour. Later theorists such as Weber attempted to remedy this by pointing out that people see themselves and are treated by others not just as economic beings, but in other ways that do not depend so much upon their economic circumstances alone as on their social identity: their general style of life, their sex, their religious membership, their educational level, their ethnic identity, or their descent, to name the most important. Of course, such 'status-groups', as Max Weber called them, may also be economically under- or over-privileged as well — may also be *classes* — but Blacks are poor in South Africa because they are confined to low-paying jobs *on racial grounds*; 'Untouchables' in India (also called Harijans or 'Scheduled Castes') on the grounds of their religious 'inferiority'; and Catholics in Northern Ireland are discriminated against in housing, education and jobs, not because they are unskilled workers, but because they are Catholics. Workers, then, don't have any monopoly of exploitation. Rather, women and ethnic minorities are especially exploited, both when they are workers and when they are not.

The working class is therefore by no means culturally or socially homogeneous, nor, whatever the degree of their economic exploitation, is position in the occupational structure the sole cause or the only source of their economic disprivilege. Even leaving aside these 'extra-economic' differences, the 'sectional' bonds that divide the working class — levels of skill, differences of industry, degree of monopolistic 'job-control', i.e. via the 'closed shop' — are as significant as those that make for interests in common *vis-à-vis* capital. Moreover, such differences are skilfully used to deliberately split the working class. Lenin, like Kautsky before him, indeed came to the conclusion that the working class, left to itself, would never develop a revolutionary consciousness, only a 'trade union' consciousness, oriented to defence and improvement of its position within capitalism. Revolutionary ideas would have to be implanted in the working class from outside by professional revolutionaries. Even trade union consciousness, however, is perfectly compatible with the exclusion of whole categories of workers on the part of privileged workers, not merely on grounds of skill-differentials and qualifications, but on quite non-economic grounds, such as the closure of lines that divide White workers from Black in South Africa. In 1922, White workers even fought police and Army with guns under banners reading "Workers of the World Unite, for a White South Africa'.

Economic stratification may or may not coincide with social stratification. Where they do coincide, as in South Africa, Blacks are separated from Whites not only at work, in the poorest jobs, but in every other social field, too: residentially, in ghetto townships; socially, via laws forbidding intermarriage or even sexual intercourse; segregated in different schools, and prevented from 'socializing' in their leisure hours — a situation sociologists have called 'status crystalization'. Blacks are low on *every* score, and there is no area of life at all where they can find partial comfort in equality or even in a limited superiority. In such 'total' situations, conflict in any one area (e.g. over schooling, housing, access to recreational facilities, or whatever) is liable to spark off opposition to the system as a whole, and violence, or the threat of it, is what keeps it going. In the Indian caste system, again, the different castes are closed off from intercourse with each other not only because they follow different occupations, the highest caste, the Brahmans, being predominantly better-off landowners in the countryside and owners, managers and professionals in the cities, the lowest, the 'Untouchables' — the street cleaners, lavatory attendants, etc. — but as in South Africa, are socially cut off from each other by rules which do not allow them to intermarry, eat together, or even touch or approach too near one another. Since one is *born* into a caste, and, in quite a different way from South Africa, the whole system is endorsed by an all-persuasive religious doctrine, one's fate in every sphere of life is determined by one's caste status.

Of the classes cited by Marx in the famous opening of the *Communist Manifesto* — 'Freeman and slave, patrician and plebeian, lord and serf, guildmaster and journeyman' — none of them are in fact, simply economic classes. They are 'extra-economic' status-groups, a fact which, at other times, Marx recognised: it was only under capitalism, he argued, that human relationships had become 'rationalized' according to a purely economic logic (though we have seen this to be by no means wholly true even of capitalism, either). If class solidarity can be fractured by such divisions within the working class, conversely there is ample evidence that as modern market relationships, industrial solidarity and social mobility become more marked, especially in the cities, caste loyalty itself is replaced increasingly by loyalty to class. Class *can* thus cut across status membership. But this is not *necessarily* so. The Church of England, for instance, traditionally contained both the squire and his tenants; the Conservative Party, likewise, still obtains the votes of no less than a third of British trade unionists. Non-economic vertical divisions thus cut across the horizontal bonds of class. Conservative theorists and practical politicians have always emphasized these vertical bonds – common identity as citizens, or as 'freeborn Englishmen' whatever one's economic fortune or lack of it; common identity as against foreigners; the 'complementary' interests of both worker and employer, and so on – just as radicals have used the same slogans to claim equality.

Vertical integration or incorporation, or the divisions within the working class, are not, however, phenomena that just 'happen'. They are *made* to happen by skilful and energetic ruling classes who monopolize the means of communication and are thereby able to influence the thinking of the less powerful. In the past, they did this via the pulpit; today, through the privately-controlled mass media. The importance of this cultural hegemony was most coherently recognized among Marxist thinkers by Antonio Gramsci, who died in Mussolini's gaols, and by his less well-known contemporary, the Peruvian José Carlos Mariátegui. Gramsci was profoundly influenced by Machiavelli's distinction between rule based on force and rule based on consent, which latter could be manufactured, and he explored the ways in which the rich exploited their power over communications to persuade the working class that the system was just inevitable or beneficial to the really deserving, together with the modern myth that the media are really open to all and not significantly controlled by the bourgeoisie. Bourgeois rule, he argued, depends quite fundamentally upon the internalization of these ideas by the working class.

Such ideas are more difficult to sell when the vast majority are plainly doing badly, and especially when they contrast their lot with that of the highly privileged. But poverty – and wealth – are always relative conceptions. Deprivation is a relative concept: we can only think of ourselves as being better or worse off in relation to others. Really poor people, though often made conscious of someone like Evita Perón or Mohammad Ali who have become extremely rich through careers outside industry or business, see little of the lives of corporation executives or merchant bankers. They are therefore normally more likely to compare their lot with those of people around them they do know at first-hand: certainly the manager, but also other categories within the working class itself with which they compare themselves invidiously: older workers *v*. younger ones; employed *v*. unemployed; men *v*. women; those who work 'un-social hours *v*. '9 to 5' employees; manual *v*. non-manual, etc. Or they turn their frustrations against groups like 'long-haired students' who seem to them unreasonably privileged, or against Blacks, who seem both inferior and a threat to the limited privileges they do enjoy. Secondly, they compare their situation with their own lives in the past, which in turn provides them with expectations about the future. Sometimes this leads to a sense of achievement and improvement, or a positive attitude to the future. But it can also lead to a 'revolution of rising expectations', which can even produce mass revolutionary discontent, not because of endemic poverty — which people have put up with for thousands of years — but where people have become accustomed to regular improvements, however slight or slow, in living standards, but suddenly find these halted.

The absence of any serious questioning of the capitalist system as a whole in the advanced capitalist world since 1945 is, conversely, scarcely unconnected with steady economic growth, which has meant rising living standards, even for the masses, as well as more upwards mobility, in an expanding economy, for increasing numbers of professionals, supervisory and white-collar workers from lower-class backgrounds. The ratio of people in tertiary employment — the vast service sector — has also increased, while the proportion of the labour force actually producing commodities has declined. Mass upward social mobility has been a fact, and even for those who didn't achieve it themselves, was a plus in favour of their society and a possibility for their children. In reality, the upper and middle class made sure that their children continued to take the lion's share of such jobs, but the method by which this was ensured is presented as one that was 'open to all' or 'open to the talents', because it is done through an education system in which secondary education is compulsory and tertiary education a mass phenomenon. Selection can now be claimed to be both rational and fair, since it is based on performance in examinations, on 'earned' credentials and on 'scientific' I.Q. tests which many believe to measure native intelligence. In Michael Young's term, the upwardly-mobile are seen as a 'meritocracy'. This mode of selection is therefore even compatible with belief in *inherited* superiority and inferiority, as racist defenders of I.Q. tests reveal, even though the overwhelming majority of social scientists, including the majority who attribute *some* credibility to the tests, conclude that performance in them, and in exams, reflects the material and immaterial advantages of privileged access to books, private schools, privacy in the home, parental stimulus and the like.

Such ideas, Gramsci argued, are part of the 'cultural hegemony' exercised by ruling classes. They are not limited to rich and expanding industrial economies, for the poor throughout history have always been taught to accept their poverty. At different times, the material privileges of the rich have been presented as divinely ordained, the outcome of 'human nature', or of the 'logic' of the market, sometimes as justified, at others as lamentable but inevitable. To people in the West, the intensity of exploitation of peasants might seem totally unacceptable and hence likely to result in endemic radicalism. But recent studies of peasants emphasize that they normally have only very modest expectations. Their 'moral economy' does include, as an irreducible minimum, however, the right to enough land to maintain their families, usually at little beyond subsistence level, and enough food to save them from starvation if the crops fail. The people who provide them with this insurance may be their neighbours — which promotes class solidarity. But since *their* crops, too, are likely to fail at the same time, or, today, because changes in world prices spell disaster for all of them, the only other resource is to the landlord, with whom they therefore maintain close 'vertical' ties, whether as a fellow-Christian or as a godparent to their children. Today, however, new cultural horizons — and therefore potential stimulus to increased acquisitiveness and discontent — are opened up by television and radio, which encourage the poor to want (and buy) more. They can also see more of the lives led by the rich. The State, too, provides a new alternative to the landlord both as employer and as a source of survival in crisis.

Most versions of Marxism suffer, then, from the inadequacy of the common model of the relationship between the economy and the rest of the social order. Though this model — of 'base' and 'superstructure' — is patently inadequate, the great strength of Marxism is that, analytically, it does focus upon material *interest*, on the economic, power and status rewards enjoyed by those who control society, and the exploitation suffered by the great majority who do the producing, and upon the mechanisms which justify these basic inequalities and which cope with resistance to them.

Both the strengths and the inadequacies are revealed in recent Marxist debate about one institution often thought of as quintessentially 'non-economic': the family. Functionalist sociologists like Parsons long ago pointed out that the family *did* service the economy: 'reproducing' the labour force and socializing children into their future roles, even relieving the tensions generated by work. Some Marxists, too, in a 'super-functionalist' way, exaggerated this degree of 'fit' between the family (and school) and the economy by labelling these 'State [sic] apparatuses'. It was left to other Marxist theorists to point out, not so much the 'complementary' way the family 'fits' the economy, or the 'relief' of tension it provides, as the ways in which all this depends upon a double exploitation of women — as workers and as housewives — and entails enhanced conflict within the family because of the contradictions generated by the stereotyped gender-roles imposed by society. The forms and functions of the family under capitalism, however, vary very considerably indeed and are the outcomes of complex and widely differing historical and cultural — including precapitalist — heritages, not just something engineered by the State or by ruthless capitalists. Why women are treated as a 'reserve army' of low-paid producers and reproducers does not derive from any necessity of the capitalist mode of production, for they have always been disprivileged. Capitalism, too, has been quite compatible with slavery, where the nuclear family was forbidden and people used as breeding-stock. It is even compatible with quite communal styles of domestic life and ways of bringing up children, as in the case of the Israeli kibbutzim.

There has to be *some* 'fit' between the family and the economy, but it can vary considerably and the fit need not be very tight. Certainly the economy 'in itself' (whatever that might mean) by no means *determines* whether descent is traced through the mother or the father, whether polygyny is preferred or forbidden, whether the State arrogates to itself the education of children, etc. It is true that capitalism places a high value on individualism and on private property, but the forms of the family that exist today depend upon historical and cultural heritages that are both very ancient and never identical from one capitalist society to another. Thus Anderson, a Marxist historian, has argued that the institutions of feudalism, in particular the division of political authority instead of its centralization, shaped British political institutions in the subsequent capitalist epoch, and that Western capitalism as a whole was profoundly shaped by institutions like the Roman system of law and the Roman Catholic Church which date from the civilizations of ancient Greece and Rome, the epoch *before* feudalism.

Weber, Marx's lifelong critic, expressed the relationship between the economic and non-economic more aptly by using the term 'affinity' rather than the more deterministic language of causality and of 'base' and 'superstructure' (a notion only used, as an image, in a few places in Marx's writings, anyhow). So while it is true that people must produce and eat in order to survive and be able to do anything beyond eating, and true, too, that society must be 'provisioned' through industry and agriculture, only an historical and cultural — not just a purely economic — analysis, can tell us why some people consume pheasant and port, others a handful of rice, and yet others witchetty grubs.

3

Social Evolution

Living in the nineteenth century, Marx and Engels were affected not only by the stirring social ideas of the eighteenth century, by the Enlightenment and the twin Revolutions, but also by the triumphs of natural science: firstly, in the sciences dealing with the inorganic — in mechanics, in chemistry, physics, and geology — and eventually in the life sciences too. It was the Darwinian revolution that stamped the thinking of the Victorians, and its methods were quickly applied to social life. Religious authority had long been practically challenged, and the rationalists had made an intellectual critique even of the *Bible*, but it was left to Darwin to formulate a theory of the emergence of life within Nature, and of the place of humanity in that process. Marx, indeed, had proposed dedicating *Capital* to Darwin. Moreover, it was not just process, but *progress*: lower forms, whether of inanimate matter, cellular organisms, or forms of society, gave way to higher ones.

Most thinkers at the time were optimists. They believed, with Comte, that humanity was now capable of using science to satisfy human needs. We were standing on the brink of a new epoch. Such optimism was as readily combined with conservatism as with radicalism: the evolutionary turning-point could be seen as beginning not in the future, when humanity as a whole would take charge of its own destiny, but now, when intelligent elites could begin to guide social life along the lines indicated by the new social science. Such a doctrine could therefore justify a range of possible arrangements from Hegel's apologia for the Prussian state to liberal reformism.

So devastating was the impact of Darwinism that procedures of natural science were taken to be the models for scientific method in general, and hence those to be applied in social inquiry too. The canons and procedures of abstraction, testing, verification or disproof — of empirical 'positive' research — would now replace mere conjecture or purely logical reasoning. If laboratory experiments might not be possible, they had not been for Darwin either. But Nature itself constituted if not one huge laboratory at least a storehouse of results, as it were, in which simpler forms of life could be studied whether in the form of still-living species or from the fossil record.

Comparative ethnology (which we call social or cultural anthropology today) was similarly considered to provide evidence of successive forms in social evolution which had emerged and become dominant, or been eclipsed and marginalized by adaptation to specialized environmental niches, or had stopped developing altogether or died out. And since Darwin had shown that the emergence of successive dominant forms was not a random process but took place according to the laws of natural selection, the search both for *laws* and stages of development in human society was now on.

Marx's conception of law, then, was naturally conditioned by nineteenth-century natural science conceptions of what a 'law' was, and by a conception of science which applied to both Nature and society and saw both as being determined by the operation of such laws. Though Marx was familiar with more probabilistic conceptions of law from his study of statistics, his more usual conception was much more deterministic and mechanistic: in a word, positivistic. In common with most Victorian writers, he usually tended to emphasize, for instance, 'the necessity of successive determinate orders of social conditions . . . both the necessity of the present order of things, and the necessity of another order into which the first must inevitably pass over'. On the other hand, he points out immediately that the laws regulating social life, unlike the laws governing Nature, were historically relative: 'Every historical period has laws of its own . . ., and in passing over from one given stage to another, it begins to be subject to other laws' (*Capital*, Vol. 1). He further recognized that there were forces which might counteract the operation of an economic 'law': trade union organization or factory legislation, for instance, which might counteract the built-in tendency of capitalism to force wages down to the lowest possible level, or that there was an 'historical element' in subsistence, i.e., as we would now say, that poverty was culturally defined and relative, not an absolute. By the time he came to write Volume 3 of *Capital*, he could observe that the 'law' of the declining rate of profit might be similarly counteracted by other social forces: more machinery ('constant' capital) might actually require *more* labour ('variable' capital), in which case, the 'law' might be only a 'tendency'. But more often he insists that 'pauperism' is 'the absolute general law of capitalism' and that though the law never operated alone, pure and undisturbed, and though its operation might be slowed down or impeded, these only offered the working class '*occasional* chances for . . . temporary improvement' (my italics).

The rise of modern physics, after Marx's death, gave rise to much more relativistic conceptions of law than those Marx used. And in the social sciences, the neo-Kantian school was to argue that social action, in any case, was different in kind from what went on in Nature, since people possessed consciousness, both individuals and groups reflected upon what they were doing and upon what was happening to them. Hence varying interpretations could be put upon the 'same' situation, drawing upon different cultural resources (ideologies, utopias, theories of all kinds). Hence it was quite fundamental, in analysing social life, to understand these *subjective* ideas, the 'meanings' that informed the behaviour of people, but which were not problematic in studying Nature, since rocks do not think and electrons never feel frustration.

These ways of thinking were familiar enough to Marx from idealist philosophy, as we saw in the quotation about the difference between spiders and humans above. But though he explicitly rejected a 'one-sided materialism', he often tended to fall back into it in his eagerness to combat the pure idealists, or into a mode of thinking which assumed that the *same* scientific methods were applicable to the study of both Nature and society.

Like other nineteenth-century social scientists from Comte to Spencer, he (rightly) insisted that societies, like organisms, were systems, composed of parts (social institutions). Each part was influenced by its relationship to the rest, and the whole was greater than the sum of the parts. But this left open the question as to whether all institutions were of equal weight, and of how the different institutions fitted one another. The search was on for a master principle analogous to natural selection in biological evolution. For idealists, the dynamic of social development was humanity's intellectual capacity. For Marx, it had to be 'material' — and he found it, eventually, in the concept of the mode of production.

If ethnology had sprung into existence because of these intellectual stimuli, the spread of capitalism across the globe had provided a sudden abundance of new information about exotic ways of life. Explorers, missionaries, and colonial administrators provided an ever-increasing flood of data out of which social philosophers constructed theories about the evolution of society and the nature of humankind.

These 'data' were inevitably interpreted in accord with evolutionist assumptions. If Melanesians or Bantu were found to accord great respect to the mother's brother, this was because they had formerly traced descent through the mother's line rather than through the father's, and, somehow, this 'custom' had got left over: it was a 'survival', like the appendix. Reasoning along these lines, every major ethnologist of the nineteenth century, Marx and Engels included, 'reconstructed' these believed stages so as to provide an overall theory of the general evolutionary progression of humankind.

Engels' *The Origin of the Family, Private Property and the State* (1884) is by far the most widely-read Marxist statement on social evolution. It is based on very wide scholarly reading, but basically draws its framework from Lewis Henry Morgan, an American ethnologist. Marx himself never produced a consolidated study of this kind, though some of his manuscripts on *Precapitalist Economic Formations* have been published. His voluminous ethnological notes, accumulated over a lifetime, have also been published, but are little studied.

It is Engels, rather, who has provided the Marxist model of the successive stages of social evolution which millions have read, though no-one reads other nineteenth-century models. The reason for this neglect of rival theories — and of Marx himself — is not simply that Engels wrote so well, whereas Marx left scrappy notes written in an extraordinary mixture of English and German even within the same sentence. Engels has always attracted readers completely uninterested in kinship in primitive society *per se* because he draws conclusions about the way in which property relationships distort sex and family relations in capitalist society, and holds out the promise of more egalitarian relationships in a future communist society.

'The history of hitherto existing society', the *Communist Manifesto* opens, 'is the history of class struggles', to which Engels added later virtually the only important amendment to the text, so crucial did he consider the point, that 'everywhere from India to Ireland . . . primitive communistic society' preceded class society.

In *The Origin of the Family* he postulates that primitive people at the dawn of human history were economically and sexually communistic. At that time, he says, ties of kinship were probably more important than economic relationships. Gradually, through a number of stages, the practice of unconstrained sex-relations became successively limited, as, firstly, only groups of brothers jointly had privileged access to groups of women, then single males to several wives, until finally modern monogamous marriage emerged. Along the way, descent, which had naturally originally been traced through the mother (for if there were many sexual partners biological paternity would be uncertain), now switched to the male line, and the former equality of the sexes, based on complementary economic roles, gave way to male control over property — including rights over women and children.

Contemporary anthropologists accord no more credibility to this flight of imaginative reconstruction than they do to the equally outmoded nineteenth-century schemes of McLennan or Lubbock. There are much more convincing explanations of the mother's brother's role, for instance, than the assumption that children once belonged to the mother's side of the family (one of the key alternative arguments being simply that the mother's side of the family is still important, and that her brother is the senior male of her generation on that side of the family). A more fundamental methodological flaw, however, derives from the assumption that societies which are egalitarian as far as access to the means of production is concerned cannot be labelled 'class' societies, though in fact they are commonly strongly stratified according to sex and age. Once again, economic relations are given special status, and inequalities based on other criteria treated as insignificant or as mere 'reflections' of the economic. But Engels' ideas have persisted, and have recently even been revived by some left-wing writers in the women's movement concerned to understand why it is that women are unequal not only under capitalism but in all class societies.

They came to the conclusion that *class* was the causal factor. Before class society, they believed, there had been epochs (still observable in 'primitive' cultures) when women had been equal in status to men and at times even superior. Unfortunately, neither belief is tenable: firstly, logically, because this still leaves open the question as to why *sex* should be transformed into gender, and why this should be the basis of inequality in such widely-differing class societies; and secondly, empirically, because even if there are significant areas in some cultures in which the contribution of women is recognized and highly valued, only most exceptionally are the crucial key decision-making posts in economic, political and religious affairs regularly held by women, as the myth of 'matriarchy' requires. This, however, still leaves Engels' passionate lines on the subjection of women under capitalism and his picture of an alternative future communist society free from gender-discrimination as appealing as ever. Further, in his own life, he did try to live according to these new principles.

Although the science-fiction of 'primitive communism' has to be put on one side, once Engels gets onto the analysis of the societies of classical Antiquity — Greece and Rome — and 'barbarian' Germanic society, where he had a much sounder grounding in the historical literature, he becomes more convincing, for he is able to demonstrate interconnections between systems of kinship, production, household organization, religious ideas, warfare, etc., and the ways in which *all* of these changed as societies originally organized on the basis of clan and tribe gradually became transformed into class societies with slave-economies, and engaged in trade, warfare and colonial conquest far outside the home country. Usually, Marx and Engels treated these transitions as total transitions: *all* institutions being transformed as one epoch gave way to another. At other times, they allowed for a certain independence of the parts. Thus art, Marx considered, might develop in ways that were only indirectly determined by economic relationships.

If 'primitive communism' was a myth, the emergence of class societies, in which the means of production — notably land and slaves — were privately owned, and the fruits of the labour of the producing class were appropriated by the owning classes, was not. The model is evolutionary in that it postulates the successive emergence of new and more complex forms of society. Within this overall evolutionary framework, however, the model had a place for revolution, for the displacement of one dominant mode of production and of the class which controlled it did not occur as a smooth transition. Old ruling classes inevitably resisted challenges to their supremacy; new ones not only had to overthrow them by force, but also to remake society across the board. The new, in Hegelian fashion, grew up within the old; the break was a qualitative rupture and the old whole was replaced by a new whole.

Marx was capable of extremely forthright political and theoretical statements about the laws which governed social development and the direction of that development, describing them as 'absolute' or 'iron' determinism. But he was also a careful scholar, even, at times, so sensitive to the need to carefully examine the evidence of the latest researches or the newest developments in society, that he never published most of his voluminous manuscripts, and constantly polished and repolished those he did publish, which caused Engels to call *Capital* 'that damned book', since it ruined Marx's life and health. Marx himself spoke of his labour as a 'nightmare'. This perfectionism and scholarly caution nevertheless also contrasted with his natural human propensity to see revolution or capitalist crisis as being around the corner, not unreasonably in 1849, though less reasonably ten years later. As the revolutionary tide of 1848 receded, too, one finds more emphasis upon the inevitability of structural contradictions built into the capitalist economy, leading to its collapse, and less on Promethean changing of the world by class action.

As far as the periodization of stages of social development and the delineation of the different modes of production were concerned, Marx became more tentative and exploratory the further back he went from capitalism and the further away from Europe. Engels was more decisive in *The Origin of the Family*: 'Slavery was the first form of exploitation, peculiar to the world of antiquity; it was followed by serfdom in the Middle Ages, and by wage labour in modern times. These are the three great forms of servitude, characteristic of the three great epochs of civilization'.

This model was based predominantly on European historical materials, the stages recognized being those of 'ancient' society, feudalism, capitalism and − eventually − socialism. At any given time, in any given society, however, there would be a 'mix' of modes of production: merchant capitalism, say, combined with both slave-estate and free peasant agriculture. But one type was predominant. Nor did they always insist that each stage must occur in ineluctable sequence: societies could either skip stages, or get stuck and go no further. They also recognized that there might have been deviations from this Europe-based sequence in other parts of the world, not only as a sequence, but also because there might have been forms of economy and society that Europe had never known. Thus Marx later in his life carefully studied Russian historical and social science literature, and came to the conclusion that the existence of the Russian village community, the *mir*, in which land was jointly owned and periodically redistributed by the community as a whole according to need, might make possible the transition to modern socialist agriculture without having to go through the stage of private capitalist agriculture, and poured scorn on rigid deterministic revolutionists: his 'historical sketch of the genesis of capitalism', he said, was not to be taken as 'an historical-philosophical theory of the general path which every people is fated to tread'.

The crucial difference between the Western World and the East, he believed, was the existence of what was called the 'Asiatic' mode of production, a notion based on interpretations by Westerners, particularly English administrators in India, who represented that society as one in which the class that dominated the economy did not dominate the State. In the great empires of the East − in Persia, Turkey, India and

China — the machinery of government was in the hands sometimes of foreigners, sometimes of military men appointed as officials, or sometimes of professional administrators like the 'mandarins' in China, who were selected by examination. Such officials might be drawn from the ranks of the landowning gentry, and might retire to their estates or be rewarded with concessions of land on their retirement, but during their term as public servants, their income was predominantly or wholly derived from their office (e.g. a share of the taxes they collected, or a stipend), not from private sources. Moreover, they were usually rotated round the empire to ensure that they did not build up a local power-base.

Such a system left decisive power in the hands of the Emperor and court at the apex of the combined administrative, political and military hierarchies — but not necessarily as representative of the landowning class. At times, Marx and Engels followed earlier writers who explained this concentration of power over huge areas in technological terms: in terms of irrigation-agriculture which was based on a system of reservoirs (the 'tanks' of India and Sri Lanka) or on a vast network of dykes, canals and feeder systems (as in China) which necessitated, in turn, it was believed, a permanent centralized system of control throughout the country, reaching into every village. Later scholars have demonstrated, however, that many of these "hydraulic" works were commonly both built piecemeal and only linked up later and that they were more often locally maintained without any need for central control by bureaucrats or kings.

At the same time — and rather contradictorily — Marx and Engels emphasized that there was a *dis*connection of levels as between life in the village and the external framework of the State. Normally, they believed, the State scarcely intervened in village life. It simply appeared, after the harvest, in the shape of the tax-collector, and then disappeared again. Within the village, the agriculturalists paid the village specialists — from the barbers to the leather-workers — in grain. So the 'little community', as later anthropologists were to call it, was seen as a self-sufficient, non-monetary, egalitarian and virtually eternal 'natural' economy, rather than as a class society (rather astoundingly, considering the importance of caste, for instance).

Like recent interpretations of Western feudal society, this idyllic picture simply omits the landlord and the economic inequalities of caste. In India, the dominant landowners were also either Brahmans or Warrior (Kshatriya) castes; in China the 'gentry'. In addition to the taxes collected by State officials, these landowners also extracted rent, in labour, in kind and in services, from those beneath them: the producers who were certainly an exploited class economically, but whose economic inferiority was only part of a more general status determined by their being *born* as an inferior category of humanity, a cosmic fate which carried with it the duty to serve their superiors; in China, the three great hierarchical relationships on which the stability and persistence of the social order was believed to depend were the deference owed by wife to her husband, a son to his father and the citizen to the Emperor. 'Extra-economic' ascription was thus fundamental.

The existence of a strong governmental bureaucracy, then, was perfectly compatible with the existence of a dominant landowning class. But the reason why this conception of Asiatic despotism has attracted enormous interest in recent years outside Asia itself, and especially in Eastern Europe, is not that people have suddenly become strangely interested in comparative history or in Asia, but that it provides explicit classical Marxist authority for the proposition that there can be a kind of class society in which those who run the State may not necessarily be those who own the means of production — here, the land. The implications are obvious: the 'political class' which runs communist society today does not own the factories and collective farms either. It is the State which juridically owns them. But sociologically, if you effectively control the State, you control the economy too — despite the formal juridical absence of private property in the means of production. And the way to join the ranks of this *ruling* (and not merely economic) class and to participate in the advantages which it offers for members, is, as for the Chinese mandarins, by entering the public/administrative apparatus, and accepting its ideology and discipline. The major difference between the communist ruling class and the Chinese mandarinate is, of course, the existence of the Party as a further 'interior' level of organization, itself controlling Government.

This model is very different from the model of the State which Marx developed for capitalism and other class societies where political power is based upon economic power. Under capitalism, though the market reigns supreme, the State in fact sees to the regulation of relations between the different interest groups and also sees to it that the economy and society as a whole does not break down because of sectional disputes between these different power groups. Today, the role of the State has grown enormously, but even in Marx's day it mattered, for, internally, there has to be a system of law and a way of enforcing judicial decisions, and, externally, a force (the Army) to defend the society against attack from outside. Finally, a societal ideology, usually religious, expressing the legitimacy of the political system and of those who control it, the rights and obligations of citizenship and of different kinds of categories of subject, plus an ethical code embodying the basic principles which ought to govern relations between citizen and State and between categories of citizens, are further prerequisites of class society, whether the codes take the form of the 'divine right of kings' or of parliamentary democracy.

Marx argued that the State — in inegalitarian class societies — would inevitably reflect the interests of whichever class had the greatest stake in the economy. Hence it would use the material power of the State — the police and the Army — above all else in order to preserve these economic rights. But he also insisted that the ruling class would also use the *cultural* machinery of courts, church, public education and communications systems to put over ideological justifications of inequality in order to persuade the mass of the people to support the system or to neutralize potential opposition: at the very least to ensure acquiescence.

Capitalists, moreover, were not all of a kind; there were different forms of capitalist property and different kinds of capitalist enterprise at different points in the cycle of production and exchange: landowners, industrialists in heavy and light industry and in service industries, merchant bankers, wholesalers, retailers and so forth and so on. In his brilliant analysis of French society, *The 18th Brumaire of Louis Napoleon*, Marx listed three 'fractions' among the bourgeoisie alone (the industrial bourgeoisie, the finance aristocracy, and the large landowners) and further refers to the 'merchant class' and the middle classes, as well as the 'petty' bourgeoisie. Nevertheless, all these 'fractions' of the bourgeoisie proper still had an overriding common interest in keeping capitalism going and keeping the workers in their place. The State — the kings, parliaments, parties, the civil service and judiciary and the established church — were the instruments through which this was done: it was a 'committee of the whole bourgeoisie'. Modern Marxists often interpret this to mean that the bourgeoisie directly manage politics — which would make it difficult to explain a Jimmy Carter or a Margaret Thatcher, of relatively humble social origins. Rather, as long as government is run in a way that does not interfere with their interests, the bourgeoisie do not need to go into politics or administration themselves: someone else can see to that while they get on with making money. At times, too, the State may even act in ways injurious to the interests of one section or other of the capitalist class.

Marx's model of the State had, of course, had to be seriously modified once organizations representing quite other social classes, especially parties of Labour, cooperatives and trade unions, entered the political arena and often, indeed, went on to form governments themselves. Modern government, too, whoever is in power, normally requires the continual involvement and consultation of the major interest groups in the political process, even under dictatorships. In pluralist political systems in the advanced capitalist countries, opposition is both legal and institutionalized: social-democratic parties normally provide the main alternative to parties explicitly in favour of the *status quo*, but interpret the interests of the classes that vote for them as requiring not the elimination of capitalism so much as its humanization. They have been the parties of Welfare and full employment. By contrast, in communist societies, not only has the capitalist class had its property expropriated, and political parties in favour of capitalism been suppressed, but no opposition parties are permitted. The nature of the ruling class, in societies without private ownership — whether, indeed, it ought to be labelled a 'class' at all — cannot be answered by using a model in which State power is assumed to be based upon private ownership of the means of production.

The handful of countries in which industrialized capitalism — Marx's 'machinofacture' — first became established and which eventually extended their power over the whole globe is not the whole of the capitalist world, however. Though capitalism took long to mature, the Industrial Revolution, once it was launched, meant, in the graphic words of one Marxist historian, that

> 'for the first time in human history, the shackles taken off the productive power of human societies, which henceforth became capable of the constant, rapid, and up to the present limitless multiplication of men, goods, and services.'
> (E. J. Hobsbawm, *The Age of Revolution, 1789–1848*).

This explosion of productive power gave Europe an edge over the rest of the world she had never before possessed. Alongside this industrial, commercial, and military triumph went new doctrines of the Rights of Man and later of the rights of the masses, and new notions of the nature of the political community, in particular the ideas of the nation and of socialism. European ideas — including the *Bible* — were taken very seriously as they presumably contained the answer as to how imperialist powers had been able to develop so effectively. The world outside Europe, by contrast, seemed incapable of offering any resistance or any viable alternative. Certainly, European imperialists treated the cultures of the world outside Europe as of little account. All the great variety of kingdoms, empires, tribes, theocracies, of gigantic armies and little bands of hunters, of religions that sought to conquer the world or to renounce it altogether, all fell before the irresistible march of capitalism. Previous history and cultures, it seemed, though they might have little in common otherwise, could simply be lumped together, residually, as 'precapitalist'.

Marx spared no crocodile tears for the elimination of the Asiatic institutions of centuries. The building of railways and factories and the establishment of plantations in the colonies would bring about not only the elimination of archaic institutions, but would also signal the beginnings of what would be a re-run, outside Europe, of the rapid construction of another set of new bourgeois societies. As in North America, the colonies would develop capitalist industry and agriculture, run by their own new bourgeoisies, who would eventually strive to become independent of London and Paris.

In reality, in Asia, capitalism did not do much transforming for centuries after the arrival of the early European traders and conquerors. European trade remained very insignificant, and production was predominantly undertaken on traditional estates or by peasant smallholders, not on capitalist plantations. Only with the expansion of industrial production and productivity in the nineteenth century, and with consequent rapidly-growing mass consumer demand back in Europe and a new drive to secure new markets abroad, did the East, in turn, begin to be thoroughly transformed along capitalist lines.

Capitalism in the colonies, however, still did not follow the scenario of modernization Marx had written, for the new capitalisms were only to be given supporting roles in the cast of the world play; the stars were to remain the established capitals of the Western world. The rest of the world was to undergo the experience of the 'development of underdevelopment': to be converted into a reservoir of cheap labour, raw materials, and high profits, and a market for the manufactured goods of industrialized worlds. India, for instance, was 'de-industrialized' and capitalist relations introduced into her agriculture. Politically, she was not to become a bourgeois state either, as, whatever the formal title, she remained a colony. Nor were social institutions transformed into carbon copies of European social institutions, based on liberal rationalism, partly because the colonial authorities were not always capable of uprooting, say, the great religions of the East; partly because it was not necessary to do so. Where they did not need to innovate, they did so ruthlessly. Radically new economic institutions, such as the slave-plantation, might be established, but were based on relationships quite different in kind from those found in capitalist enterprises back in Europe. In the older colonies, notably in Latin America and the Caribbean, entire new racist social orders were brought into existence over the centuries, and Christian institutions and beliefs ruthlessly imposed. The outstanding innovation was slavery: the exploitation of supremely unfree, 'extra-economically' exploited labour. These massive changes, too, were accomplished by the State, not merely via the operation of the market, as when millions of peasants were transformed into Christians and workers in the gold and silver mines of Peru and Mexico.

The relationship between State and economy, the kind of cultural order introduced, and the basic relationships in production itself thus all varied considerably. Though the world market was very definitely now a capitalist one, production was often organized on very different lines from those of the classical Marxist model of the proletarian bound to his master by the cash nexus.

The 'Great Transformation', as Karl Polanyi called the European bourgeois economic and social revolutionary watershed at the beginning of the nineteenth century, had thus sparked off, in its turn, a second great transformation, this time across the globe. But what it produced, in what was to eventually be labelled the Third World, was not the industrial society that Marx at one time thought it would, but a *dependent* capitalism. It was this relationship of *multiple* inferiority — of economic exploitation resulting from political domination, and endorsed by racism, imperialism and chauvinism — that was to prove a much more explosive mixture than the purely economic conflicts that Marx had emphasized in his analysis of the advanced capitalist countries. Capitalism did not collapse as a world-system, nor, where it did break down, did it do so in the heartlands of capitalism: in England, in Germany, in Holland or in France. Socialism was to be established, instead, initially in backward countries, the first being a very large European country, Tsarist Russia, which, for Marx, had always been the epitome of an archaic social system and autocratic polity which guaranteed a predominantly precapitalist agrarian economy.

It had not been unreasonable to expect capitalism to break down in the West, for the advanced capitalist countries were indeed racked with endemic problems in the nineteenth century as today: boom and slump, mass poverty and mass protest were part of the normal functioning of economies that, by the end of the century, seemed likely to issue in revolution and in socialism of some kind. Why this did not occur was because 'polarization' did not occur either. Despite the distress of millions, other millions were better off than their forefathers had imagined possible. Many of the worst-off made new lives by emigrating to expanding countries, the northern European poor to the USA or Australia or South Africa; the southern Europeans to Argentina and

Brazil; and the Chinese poor around the whole Pacific. Those in regular employment were eventually even to be insured against the unpredictable disasters of sickness and unemployment. And if the worst came to the worst, force was used freely against those who did threaten to challenge the system as a whole: the IWW 'Wobblies' in the USA; the 'Reds' on the Clyde; or the anarchists and syndicalists in France, Spain and Italy.

In the end, vertical national identities were to prove infinitely stronger than horizontal and internationalist class solidarity. Lenin, in his classic essay on *Imperialism*, written in 1915, had emphasized that the sectionalist chauvinism that Marx and Engels had noted even in their lifetimes could be used both to divide the workers within a country and to link them to the capitalist class, and thereby divide the workers of one country from another. Though the real interests of the proletariat, in a worldwide economic system like capitalism, were still theoretically conceived of as inherently calling for *inter*nationalism, Lenin was writing with the actual experience of World War I behind him, when the workers of each European country had in fact marched off to fight for their respective bourgeois masters against the proletarians of other countries. He knew, too, how weakly-rooted capitalism was in Russia, though he continued to emphasize the likelihood — indeed, the necessity — of a revolution in advanced countries, without which revolutions in the backward countries would be stifled and would be incapable of creating socialism. Yet it was in the backward countries — despite Marx — that the contradictions of world capitalism were most marked.

In *Imperialism*, Lenin attempted to construct a theory of why this had come about. He started from an economic assumption, founded upon Marx's distinction between 'constant' and 'variable' capital: that owing to the 'law' of the declining rate of profit in the heartlands of capitalism, because of the ever-increasing cost of unending improvements in technology, capitalism (with its built-in drive to maximize profits) sought them where labour could be bought cheapest. In the colonies, 'super'-profits were possible. Back in the homelands of imperialism, part of this enhanced profit extracted from Asia, Africa and Latin America could be passed on to a favoured 'labour aristocracy', which would therefore be inclined to find capitalism more tolerable. He did not observe, theoretically, that these superprofits were made possible because of political domination of the colonies rather than by virtue simply of economic processes, but he did come to realize, in his last years, that it would be reaction to imperialist exploitation *in the colonies* that would threaten the entire capitalist world-system.

Nationalist anti-colonialism did indeed become worldwide between the two World Wars. But although it eventually gave birth to a whole series of politically independent capitalist countries, especially after 1945, they were still economically dependent ones. Socialist revolution in the Third World was to take far longer, and when it did finally occur, it did so because economic exploitation was overlaid by other kinds of oppression: by racism and by national oppression. The stage was set for the conquest of political power by communist parties in the Third World, only when the social protest of classical Marxism became yoked to a national cause — when the communist could claim to be defending the interests of most classes, including those of the 'national' bourgeoisie, who, unlike 'comprador' capitalists who worked with and for foreign companies, were competing with them — and, above all, when they could also claim to be defending the interests of the largest and most exploited class of all, which, unlike Europe, was the peasantry rather than the tiny proletariat. This finally occurred for the first time in the largest country on earth, in China, in 1949.

4

Socialism:
Ideal and Reality

The Bolsheviks had cause to be somewhat irritated by Marx when they came to power in 1917, for there was very little in his writings that told them how to actually build and run a socialist society — especially in a ruined and backward country. Marx was strongly against what he regarded as crystal-ball gazing: socialism was something that would come about in the future, he said, and it would only be the people of the future who could work it out best, in the light of conditions no one could foresee today. But he did outline the basics, especially in the light of the lessons of the brief seizure of power by the people of Paris during the 'Commune' of 1870-1. Later he enunciated certain key changes that would be needed in *The Critique of the Gotha Programme* (a draft programme put forward in 1875 with the purpose of creating a united workers' party in Germany). In criticizing the ideas of followers of Lassalle he was led to clarify his own ideas on the transition of socialism and on the institutional bases of socialism. It would be essential not just to nationalize industry, the banks, and other key productive resources, but to dismantle the *political* apparatus of the bourgeois State, too — the Army, police, civil service, judiciary, and so on. To destroy capitalism, the power of the people in arms would be needed. The emphasis was upon the proletariat and upon mass political action such as the general strike, rather than upon the part to be played by professional revolutionaries and the structures they created. The building of socialism equally, after the taking of power, would require the unlocked energies of millions working in free association.

Marx, of course, did not spend the whole of his life in the British Museum. He flung himself into the defence of the defeated Communards and other international movements. But he by no means had it all his own way in those organizations. He encountered strong opposition both from the anarchists, at that time a revolutionary force quite as significant (or insignificant) as the communists, and, on the Right, from the much more numerous followers of a succession of political leaders from Proudhon to Lassalle, whom Marx denounced as idealist and reformist. After Marx's death, new kinds of opposition to his ideas arose, this time, however, within the ranks of those who thought of themselves as his disciples, but who nevertheless wanted to significantly modify his model. Eduard Bernstein, for instance, the man who inherited Marx's literary legacy from Engels, argued that the breakdown of capitalism was not inevitable. Nor was class polarization, in particular the disappearance of the middle classes and the peasantry. And now that the masses had become enfranchised in the advanced capitalist countries, revolution was not necessary either, for capitalism could gradually be reformed into a humane and workable 'social democracy'. The name 'Social Democrat', however, continued to be used by all, including Marxists, who identified with the cause of the workers and who stood for economic equality in addition to the formal equality of the citizen accorded by the liberal-bourgeois State. Only after 1917 was it applied as a term of contempt to 'reformist' socialists alone, and the name 'communist' thenceforth reserved for Marxist revolutionaries, and then only for those accepted as such by the Comintern controlled by the USSR.

On the Left, Marx had found much more revolutionary people than himself — advocates of revolution *now*, and advocates of terror who sought to 'destabilize' society by killing Tsars and generals and by making life insecure for everybody. But his most virulent revolutionary opponents were the anarchists, led by Mikhail Bakunin. To them, injustice, inequality and exploitation were not the result of private property or of economic classes alone, but, more widely, arose where-ever there were inequalities of *any* kind, including unequal access to power, particularly power over the institutions governing society as a whole, but also in any other kind of organisation and *including* revolutionary organizations.

The kind of organization, and the alternative society Marx wanted, the anarchists argued, would only result in a new kind of state and a new kind of class society, in which the owners of private property would not be in the saddle, but the leadership of a party monopolizing power in both Party and society, and organized from the top downwards. Instead, they argued, society should be decentralized: each factory, farm and community should run its own affairs, with everyone participating and cooperating. The State, above this level, should simply be made to disappear.

These views, today, might seem unrealistic and therefore unlikely to take on. But they did, especially in southern Europe, amongst peasants in Andalusia, skilled artisans in France and independent craftsmen like Swiss watchmakers, who were often quite militant, being threatened by competition from large-scale capitalist factories or estates, but completely lacked experience of large-scale organizations that produced a more collectivistic psychology among factory workers. Anarchist ideas took root so effectively that Marx often found himself in the minority. His response was typically decisive: he was prepared to break up the First International (the International Working Men's Association) rather than let it get into the hands of the anarchists, by shifting its headquarters to New York, a disastrous move for a movement mainly based in Europe. Similarly he got Bakunin, who was indeed infected with dangerous conspiratorial and terrorist ideas, expelled from the IWA.

Marx had concluded, after the 1848 revolutions and the Paris Commune of 1871, that the socialist revolution could only be made by the people in arms. Communists had no interests other than the interest of the working class, to which they were totally dedicated. But since they possessed a 'scientific' understanding of what those interests were and were therefore specially equipped to see clearly the direction in which society was tending, they were not, as the actual proletariat were, likely to be affected by 'false' consciousness: by utopian, anarchist, reformist or romantic super-revolutionary ideas. Hence though Marx and Engels genuinely celebrated the self-movement of the proletariat and democracy within the movement, this distinction as between the communist revolutionaries and the actual proletariat was to be the germ from which the idea of a communist leadership or 'vanguard', organized into a Party separately from the mass organizations of the proletariat, and even more so from the unorganized masses was to grow very rapidly.

The ideology of complete identification with the working class concealed the reality: a handful of self-appointed leaders, mainly, like Marx, non-proletarian 'intelligentsia' only accountable to themselves and with only tenuous connection with mass organizations. The Communist League, between 1847 and 1852, for instance, had only some 300 members.

In tiny circles like these, issues of control and responsibility did not have much significance for society as a whole — yet. But by the time of Marx's death, the first mass political party to call itself 'Marxist' — the Social Democratic Party of Germany — had already effectively become not only the party of the working class of that country, but by 1911 the largest party in the whole of Germany (twice as large as the next largest, the Catholic Centre Party), with 110 deputies in the Reichstag (Parliament), many millions of members in the trade unions affiliated to the Party, and a whole panopoly of women's sections, youth sections, holiday organizations, and social clubs, all so highly organized that they have been described as a 'state within a state'. In such a broad mass movement, advocates of reform within capitalism, notably Eduard Bernstein, soon appeared, both within the leadership and amongst the rank and file. The leadership remained loyal to the principles of Marxism, on paper at least, and, indeed, often rigidly so. This ideological purity was symbolized and apparently guaranteed, by Karl Kautsky, who took over the role of Engels, after the latter's death, as editor and interpreter of Marx's literary legacy. Today, Kautsky is known to most Marxists only as a 'renegade', for that is what Lenin called him when he went along with the German SPD in 1914 in joining the imperialist World War and later in denouncing the Bolshevik Revolution.

Today, therefore, he is ignored. Significantly, his great work on *The Agrarian Question* remains untranslated into English. But for the generation before 1914, Kautsky had been the authoritative ideological voice of Marxism in the very country where most revolutionaries now expected the revolution to occur. Only a handful within the leadership, notably Karl Liebknecht and Rosa Luxemburg, consistently queried this orthodoxy from a revolutionary point of view, both in their theoretical critiques and in their practical political activity. Luxemburg, for instance, was critical of growing parliamentarism and advocated a 'mass strike' of the whole working people to bring down capitalism, and was highly suspicious of tendencies towards oligarchy among the leadership and towards chauvinistic nationalism among the working class.

In the official ideology of the Party, it saw itself as the agency which would end capitalism and liberate the workers, opening up a new kind of class*less* society altogether different in kind from *any* kind of class rule — and therefore ushering in a new era in which humanity as a whole, for the first time since 'primitive' communism, would be free and equal. But modern communism would be based on advanced technology and upon new kinds of human beings, free from the individualism and competitiveness bred in them by capitalism, and highly motivated to work and produce for the common good of all from which they would also individually benefit. They would therefore be positively keen to raise productivity, to introduce and accept innovations, whether new technology or improved ways of working, and — most important of all — able and keen to contribute their own ideas, inventions and ways of organizing work, based on practical experience combined with new theoretical knowledge gained through education, which would be open to all. All of this would result in an undreamed of explosion of production and productivity, which in turn meant that society would be able to easily satisfy not only the basic needs of everybody, but that there would no longer be an economy of scarcity, in which only a few could live at high standards of consumption, but one in which ever-expanding wants could also be satisfied.

But Marx's vision of communism was not couched simply in terms of ever-increasing material consumption. The mere satisfaction of basic animal *needs*, or even the satisfaction of expanding material *wants* was not the end of human evolution, but only the beginning of a truly human society, in which the millennial preoccupation with material needs — with hunger, survival, shelter — would be replaced by the satisfaction of both material and immaterial wants in a society no longer divided into those who worked and those who worked with their brains. Everbody would do some of each, according to their choice: life in the town and in a modernized countryside would be equally rich and rewarding, in all senses. Alienation, then, would disappear. In a rather gentlemanly and 'pastoral' vision, written in his younger years, Marx had envisaged the communism of the future as allowing people to fish in the morning, hunt in the afternoon, and 'criticize' (philosophize) after dinner. A modern version of this vision is the Chinese notion that although they have abolished capitalist ownership, 'three great differences' — between town and country, industry and agriculture, and between manual and mental labour — remain to be abolished. (Engels would probably also have added — and the contemporary women's movement would put in first place — the abolition of the massive inequalities between men and women).

The proletariat was thus to be the agency of general human liberation, not a force setting up yet another form of class society for its own sectional benefit, even if that section might be the majority in society. Yet after the Commune Marx recognized that bourgeois resistance would be fierce: force would have to be met with force. In this emergency period of transition, the proletariat would have to exercise a 'dictatorship' to prevent counter-revolution. The expected economic expansion, he recognized, would also necessarily take a long time. Nor would workers conditioned by capitalist 'possessive individualism' become altruistic and collectivistic overnight. There would therefore have to be a transitional period before true communism could be fully established. (Later communists were to call the first stage 'socialism' and the second 'communism' proper — though Marx himself used these terms interchangeably.) Having no direct experience of mass socialist organizations, Marx did not give much thought to the nature of the party of the working class or regard it as problematic; dismissing Bakunin's charge that communism was 'the negation of liberty' on the grounds that 'self-government' would solve the problem of 'despotic' power.

The working class itself, like Prometheus, would achieve its own liberation by wresting power from those who had monopolized it, and using it for the benefit of humanity. As for the Party, it would be a class organization, merely a servant of the exploited majority, dedicated to abolishing class society altogether — and therefore different in kind from the parties of the other classes, which merely defended sectional and minority privilege. It would only have the role of formulating policy for the movement as a whole and of representing it as a whole, and maintaining an overall internationalist strategy.

Once a mass Marxist party did emerge — in Germany — however, the gap between this theory and actual reality was to present itself increasingly in the form of a growing gap between the leadership and the rank-and-file of the membership, and between the programmatic commitment to revolution and the actual incorporation of the working class and its party.

Naturally, the opponents of the German SPD were the severest critics of its claim to be more truly democratic than bourgeois parties. Yet there was growing criticism within the Party, too. Roberto Michels' book *Political Parties* (1911) was in fact predominantly a study of the SPD itself, of which he was a member. It showed the way in which the full-time leadership were becoming an oligarchy — something, he believed, that was likely to happen in all mass parties — imposing policy from the top downwards, rather than spokesmen expressing the views of the mass membership, a conclusion summed up in his famous 'iron law': 'Whoever says organization, says oligarchy'. Moreover, the Party had become adapted to the capitalist order within which it had grown up, a permanent opposition within capitalism, rather than a force dedicated to the revolutionary overthrow of capitalism.

He was not, as is often thought, a total pessimist about the possibility of democracy. He believed, rather, that such organizations went through cycles: initially closely responsive to the influence of their memberships, with high levels of participation; then settling down under oligarchic control – which in turn produced a reaction in the form of another surge of democratization. It was a model, then, with a place both for determinism and voluntarism, for the tragedy of human imperfectibility and the heroism of human will, ideals, and effort.

A parallel critique was developed by enemies of Social Democracy, notably by the sociologist Max Weber, as part of a much wider and deeper theory of history and society. Paradoxically, he extended one of Marx's own lines of thought, but turned it against socialism. In *Capital* Marx had concentrated on demonstrating how capitalism entailed the rationalization of the economy. He had also pointed out that this was accompanied not only by the emergence of Protestantism, but also by a concomitant rationalization of the rest of social and intellectual life. He did not develop the insight very far, however. But Weber did – though he refused to accept that the spirit of capitalism originated in economic relationships. Rather, for him, the intellectual, emotional and ethical attitudes appropriate to capitalist growth were of religious provenance. Protestantism, particularly Calvinism, laid the responsibility for a person's fate on their own efforts in this world, rather than on deference to the authority of the organized Church or giving priority to the purely religious life by withdrawing from the world (e.g into monasteries, or by turning holy man and begging for a living), or, for most people, through preoccupying oneself predominantly with the next life by living as non-secular Christian life as possible on this earth. The ideal and ideas informing the new religion, on the contrary, thus involved a new rationale for secular conduct. Though intended as religious rules, they were nevertheless particularly conducive to hard work, and to hard saving and to reinvestment rather than consumption. Similarly, the codification of 'bourgeois' law followed coherent unifying principles, as did the displacement of religion by science; even, in Weber's view, the shift from polyphony in medieval music to harmony in Baroque times- all evinced the same parallel tendency – the rationalization of everything. Weber saw all this, then, as a general process which certainly involved the rationalization of the economy, but only as a part of a wider tendency. The economy, that is, did not *cause* rationalization in other domains of life. It, itself, was becoming rationalized, along with everything else.

Modern economic organizations, and governmental machines, he argued, were increasingly run in accordance with explicit rational principles, not according to custom, secular or religious, or the whims of the powerful, and rights and duties at all levels were clearly specified. They were also pyramidal structures: they required obedience by those at lower levels to their superiors, but also required that those superiors themselves behave in accordance with socially-established principles; thus officials must never allow personal interests or connections, or private beliefs, to influence their work: the rules were there to be followed, and they applied to everyone irrespective of their status or wealth, etc. A pure logic thus governed every possible contingency and specified how it should be handled in the form of detailed laws and regulations.

In the political sphere, his most crucial blow was to apply this type of analysis not only to the Prussian bureaucracy, the instrument of bourgeois rule, but equally to its major opponent, the German SPD, which Weber, like Michels, saw as increasingly oligarchic since it, too, was affected by the general rationalizing process in capitalist society of which it was a part. If such a party were to come to power, Weber added, it would monopolize power, by eliminating other parties and controlling all other organizations, and thereby become a singularly terrifying instrument of total and pitiless social as well as political control.

This did not, in fact, come to pass in Germany. The militant Marxists in the leadership were only a small minority, easily defeated by the 'revisionists' who eventually cooperated with the bourgeoisie in leading the German working class into the imperialist war of 1914. After the war, the leaders of the revolutionary communist minority, Rosa Luxemburg and Karl Liebnecht, were murdered by right-wing officers. And in the end, it was neither social democracy nor communism which came to power, but Nazism.

But communism did come to power in Russia, where the ruthless Tsarist autocracy had suppressed any democratic tendency whatsoever, let alone socialism. In 1905, mass revolution broke out, both in the countryside where the majority of the population lived and in the cities. Concessions had to be made to bourgeois democracy: a kind of Parliament (the Duma) was set up, though it was no representative Parliament, since the nobles, 1% of the population, had over half the seats reserved for them. In industry, the rapidly-growing capitalist class was given its head, and a belated land reform began in the countryside. But it all came too late: the Bolsheviks — it should be noted — spread democratic as well as socialist revolutionary ideas in the Army, which was made up of peasants. These peasant-soldiers now stopped obeying their officers and instead elected their own; stopped fighting, and went home, where they began to take over the land. In February 1917, the reformist Social-Democrats who, with their allies, commanded majority support, seized power. Eight months later, they themselves were displaced by the Bolsheviks.

Anarchists apart, revolutionary movements in Tsarist Russia from terrorists to Marxists, had been underground movements, highly centralized and disciplined, demanding obedience and self-sacrifice, and rarely able to practise the open democracy of branch meetings. Party congresses had to be held in other countries. Dialectically, Tsarism stamped a centralized and authoritarian style of organization on its very opponents. By 1917, the Bolsheviks had undoubtedly succeeded in gaining the support of the majority of the urban working class. But the industrial proletariat was of very recent growth, and, in any case, was a mere 3½ million in a population of 125 million and concentrated mainly in two cities, Moscow and St Petersburg. Outside these cities, Russia was a sea of peasants in which the Bolsheviks had virtually no organization: in 1916, they had four rural branches, and in the Smolensk *guberniya*, with a population of more than two million people, had only some 10 000 members four years after the seizure of power in 1917.

The peasants, however, were also ready for revolution, though theirs was a quite different 'parallel' revolution to the coup by the Bolsheviks in the two main cities. Millions of peasants had died as soldiers. Now they wanted their reward – the land – and they took it.

Fourteen capitalist Powers invaded the infant USSR to crush the new Soviet state. Millions died of famine in the ensuing civil war and after it. In the end, the tiny working class which had supplied so many class-conscious Bolshevik 'cadres' to the Red Army had been virtually wiped out, and the task of mobilizing the population, firstly, for sheer survival, and later for the construction of a new socialist order, placed the highest possible premium upon control and organization. The economy was in chaos: most of the industrial plant was destroyed, and the peasantry was sitting tight on its newly-won tiny farms. Since prices were kept down by the Bolshevik government to keep the living costs of the growing urban population down, peasants simply stopped selling their surplus grain and meat on the market altogether.

The Communists had long advocated the technical modernization of agriculture via large, new socially-owned farms, worked by tractors in lieu of the primitive peasant smallholdings where most people farmed with wooden tools. Some advocated going very slowly, lest production decline even further; others, the immediate collectivization of the land

and an instant switch-over to mechanized agriculture. Collectivization, gradual or rapid, was put off during the period of the New Economic Policy (NEP), when private peasant production was encouraged instead. But the limitations of this form of agriculture meant continuing shortages in the cities, which, the radical wing continued to argue, could only be overcome by switching to large-scale socialist agriculture. In the end, the debate was resolved under crisis conditions, when the Bolsheviks abolished private property in land overnight and forced the peasants — sometimes at machine-gun point — to hand over their surplus grain and to join large new collective farms.

This policy was carried through by Stalin after Lenin's death. He was later to show the same ruthlessness in dealing with any other kind of opposition. In the end, dictatorship was to be used not just against bourgeois counter-revolution, but against life-long Bolsheviks: practically every member of the Central Committee was to die and millions of less distinguished Soviet Citizens sent to appalling forced labour camps. Yet Stalin had come to power not as an extremist, but as an 'organization man' who commanded effective majority support, and was seen as representing the middle way. Marxists agonized by this experience now had to ask themselves how this had been possible in a 'democratic centralist' organization: how centralism had won out over democracy. Their opponents pointed to the elimination of pluralism — of checks and balances embodied in independent institutions from courts of law to free trade unions. Marxists, however, were still reluctant to accept this 'bourgeois—liberal' critique, and tried to develop other kinds of explanation for the horrors of Stalinism.

Yet Stalin had been able to develop the support that he needed in his bid for total power because — as General Secretary — he controlled the machinery of communication within the Party and therefore had a nation-wide network of contacts at his disposal, and by appointing his supporters to the key posts in the Party machinery, especially as District Secretaries, was soon able to control the Party Congresses.

By 1940, Russia had become an industrial country, capable of defeating even Germany, a very advanced industrial Power commanding the resources of occupied Europe. By 1945, the USSR was the second most powerful country in the world. But the price had been horrific — mass terror and totalitarian control over every aspect of life. On the eve of the Revolution, in his *State and Revolution*, Lenin had repeated and developed the classical Marxist scenario — and he had genuinely meant it. Socialism would lead to the abolition of repressive control by the State over the people characteristic of class society and replace it by greater democracy: by the thorough-going participation of the workers and the peasants in the running of society. Every cook, he wrote, would rule the state. Running society, anyway, he argued, was really an 'extraordinarily simple' business of 'book-keeping and control' 'within the reach of anybody who can read and write and knows the first four arithmetical rules'. Once the class enemy had been eliminated and the new socialist economy got under way, the second stage of socialism — 'communism' proper — would begin, and the State would simply 'wither away'.

Something like that seemed to be actually happening in 1917, when 'soviets' (committees) of revolutionary workers, soldiers and sailors took over the running of the factories and the cities, replacing the existing civic authorities as well as capitalist owners and managers. Against a background of the total collapse of authority, new experiments in every sphere of life, from industry to the arts, were not only possible but inevitable and necessary. But civil war and economic chaos soon put paid to all that. Faced with serious resistance and possible anarchy, or defeat, the Bolshevik Party became converted into a ruthless machine, concentrating all power into its hands: trade unions were not allowed to strike, the soviets were converted into orthodox organs of local government under Party and central government control, and opposition parties were abolished.

Bakunin's prophecy that the strengthening of the State under socialism would inexorably lead to yet another kind of a society possibly more authoritarian than liberal-capitalist society seemed to have been tragically validated when, half a century later, his ideological descendants, the anarchists in the USSR, carried their opposition to growing Bolshevik power over the State to the point of rising in arms, in Kronstadt, against the new regime, in 1921, and were gunned down.

As we have seen, Rosa Luxemburg had feared that the Party leaderships could become much more powerful than the mass of the rank and file (though she had feared the *reformism* of such leaderships just as she believed in the inherently revolutionary potential of the masses); Michels had predicted that the centralized revolutionary mass party would give rise to oligarchy; and on the Right, Weber had prophesied that the elimination of all opposition within the Party would lead to the elimination of all opposition in society as a whole if a Party of this kind were to take power. As Stalinism grew under communism, and fascism under capitalism, even more right-wing theorists in Italy, drawing upon the ideas of Machiavelli and wedding them to *laissez-faire* liberalism, developed increasingly influential models which purported to explain why the major movement for human emancipation had turned into a repressive regime.

Vilfredo Pareto argued that all societies and all institutions, even those claiming to be democratic, were in reality governed by minorities — 'elites' — composed of the most capable people in their respective fields. Ambitious counter-elites aiming at dislodging the present incumbents and taking over power for themselves tried to build up support by appealing to 'justice', 'reason', etc. But all this was so much rhetoric — basically mere 'fraud'. Once in power, they forgot about those ideals to such a point that they came eventually to depend upon force instead. Then new counter-elites arose to challenge them ... and so on, in an eternal cycle. It was basically a psychologistic theory, based on the notion that there were different kinds of people, different *by nature*, — those endowed with tendencies to use cunning and those tending to use force in the pursuit of power — and the rest, who were merely manipulable 'masses'.

Pareto's contemporary, Gaetano Mosca, argued that it was not satisfactory to talk about elites in general: it was the 'governing elite' that was the vital one in political life. To be effective, no governing elite could rule on its own; it needed a wider social base — the support of classes below it. Sheer oligarchy was less effective than a government which could command the consent of at least a significant section of the most powerful strata outside the circles of government itself, and through them rally to their side even sections of the masses. Initially, the Bolsheviks had commanded mass support, since they stood for equality and fraternity. By the 1930s, the regime was relying mainly on terror directed against the masses, and had outlawed opposition of any kind in any area of social life, from the arts to the factory floor. Mosca and Pareto seemed to make increasing sense to theorists who now developed more sociological models of 'mass society', arguing that totalitarian rule did not come about simply because some people were by nature authoritarian and ambitious and others acquiescent, but because social structures had been broken down: with the growing power of large-scale organizations, particularly of the State itself, the older primary groups of family neighbourhood were now 'penetrated' by the State, and secondary associations, from trade unions to professional bodies, no longer had the autonomy or power needed to check those who controlled the State — and thereby, through the schools, the educational moulding of the new generation, and through the censored mass media, the minds of their parents.

Stalin had not only crushed resistance inside the USSR; he had also converted Lenin's internationalist principle that foreign Communist Parties defend the USSR into an unquestioning and total loyalty enforced upon all Communist Parties, requiring them effectively to endorse everything done by the Soviet Union. Defence of the USSR now became the first requirement of any true Communist, and only the small Trotskyite opposition developed a Marxist critique of Stalinism. Trotsky himself, a central figure in the Russian Revolution, was naturally unprepared to recognize that the reasons for the degeneration of the Revolution might include the 'democratic centralist' machinery of the Party itself, or that a whole range of other policies – agricultural policy, the strategy of rapid industrialization, the elimination of rival parties, the suppression of soviets and trade unions which acted in defiance of Party policy and their replacement by Party-controlled ones – which he and Lenin, and not only Stalin, had accepted and ruthlessly applied at different times might have been wrong not only in practice but in principle. Rather, he concentrated on another key aspect: the historic tragedy of socialist revolutionaries coming to power in a backward country, and the subsequent failure of a supporting revolution to emerge in any advanced capitalist country. Russia had then, he argued, been thrown onto its own wretched economic resources, further disastrously reduced by war and by economic collapse. Under these conditions of appalling scarcity and rationing, and of forced-draught modernization, resort to rigid control in every sphere of life was inevitable, initially to ensure not so much the construction of socialism as sheer survival. For socialism to be possible, he believed, the revolution would have to spread abroad, especially to developed countries, and eventually to the whole world. Secondly, 'inner-Party' democracy would have to be restored within the Soviet Communist Party, though the dictatorship of the proletariat – in fact, of the Party – over society as a whole was not questioned.

Despite the brilliance of his study of *The History of the Russian Revolution*, then, the critique stopped short of any serious questioning of the basic institutional arrangements and policies developed under Lenin which had spawned the monster of Stalinism. It was, however, a superior explanatory model to that developed by Stalin's successors twenty years later, after the latter's death in 1953, which largely attributed the horrors of the whole epoch to him and to an unexplained 'cult of personality', without examining the social conditions which gave rise to dictatorial rule, in a way far more reminiscent of the (bourgeois) 'great man' theory of history than of Marxism.

Equally unsatisfactory from a sociological point of view, was the Right-wing 'theory' that a bunch of mass murderers and psychotics had somehow got into power, a notion which entirely omits the organizational legacy of Tsarism which Leninism grew out of, the distinctive ideological subscription of the Bolsheviks to socialist and democratic values and goals, and the gigantic organizational problems that the latter faced in trying to bring socialism into being in such a country: in particular, as Trotsky emphasized, in *only one country*, which, large as it was, was now cut off from trade with the rest of the world, and from any significant outside aid, financial, political, moral, or whatever. The USSR found itself in quarantine, an international leper, and had to fall back on its own resources, mainly human.

Mobilizing the population involved much more than the merely negative repression of opposition. People were also positively required to do things – to work hard, to accept austerity and privation, to do what the Party, which claimed to embody and express the moral authority of the 'will of the people', told them to do. The Communist Party was therefore a completely different kind of organization from bourgeois parties, which are largely electoral organizations. Back in 1903, Lenin had fought a fierce battle with Martov over precisely this issue, when the Russian Social Democrats, as the communists were still called, were still a tiny sect. At the Party Congress of that year, Martov had argued that anyone should be allowed to join if they agreed with Party policy: it would, in this way, become a *mass* Party. Lenin, more influenced by the example of earlier Russian revolutionary sects, emphatically rejected this view. Lenin's views prevailed, though – contrary to popular legend – the Mensheviks themselves came round to fully agree with him three years later (what really divided them, rather, was the quite 'revisionist' strategy Lenin adopted soon after 1905 – though he did not pioneer it – of moving from bourgeois to proletarian revolution). Party members, both factions agreed, had to be dedicated 'professionals', putting the revolution before everything else, even life itself, and doing what they were told to do. (A later communist, a minor figure called Levin, once expressed this spirit of dedicated self-sacrifice in the interests of the Party well when he said that communists should regard themselves as sentenced to death – at the hands of the class enemy – in advance.) The lower levels of the Party – the branches or 'cells' – were indeed entitled to join and should join in the process of formulating policy, but once a decision had been taken at a higher level, particularly at the highest level – the periodic Congresses of the Party – individual members must not only accept those decisions and carry them out, but also not form 'factions' to continue fighting for the policies they had failed to secure support for, nor should lower-level organs – branches or districts. More than that, as in most democratic organizations, they must publicly defend the victorious policies they had fought *against*, since these were now official Party policy. Though Lenin certainly retained his belief in debate within the Party, the power of the leadership, with organs of communication in their hands, to determine the lines that debate was to take, and even its very outcome, was to result in the replacement of intra-Party democracy by the iron rule of one man who controlled the Party machine, and used that machine to govern the country. The dictatorship of the proletariat was thus successively replaced firstly by the dictatorship of the Party, and then by the dictatorship of Stalin over the Party.

Party members, moreover, were required to do much more than merely *accept* Party policy — mentally, as it were. They had to be constantly active promoting and spreading the Party's official policy — the 'Party line' — on every issue and in every area of life, through personal discussions, in public meetings, and by disseminating Party literature — books, pamphlets, newspapers, journals. They were also expected to match their personal performance to Party ideals by leading others, by their exemplary behaviour as 'model' workers in production and as trade union 'militants', as leaders in civic and neighbourhood organizations, in women's organizations, youth organizations, and so on. The Party line was further reinforced in every newspaper, magazine and work of art. In this way, no area of life remained free from the control of the Party.

An organization of this kind was vastly better coordinated, and therefore vastly more effective than the opposition to it. It is still the fundamental model not only for communist parties elsewhere, even those now critical of the Soviet Union, but also for 'Trotskyist' organizations and even non-Marxist — even anti-Marxist — 'liberation movements' and ruling parties in one-party states which have borrowed this organizational structure because they see it as the best way to build a powerful political force. It is by virtue of its organizational effectiveness that so many of these movements have grown and even come to power.

But the Party does not just mobilize people: it appeals to them to work for a *cause* — to eliminate repression and poverty and to construct an alternative socialist society, and to defend that society against internal opposition and external threat.

Like any political regime, the popularity of communist governments depends upon their capacity to deliver their promise of a better life. Comparisons between living standards in the West and those in Eastern European countries are usually assumed to unambiguously demonstrate the obvious superiority of the former. The ubiquity of the queue in Moscow and Warsaw is testimony enough to the reality of those differences. Yet all these countries, Czechoslovakia apart, were agrarian in 1945, and have become industrialized, as well as North

Korea; their general living standards are vastly superior — for the *whole* population — than they were before the communist era; and the 'social wage' — the network of non-monetary benefits — is in many ways superior to the Welfare State of the West. Further, they are much more open 'meritocracies' than Western countries. Being expanding economies, they have needed masses of new managers, administrators and professionals of all kinds. Social mobility on an enormous scale has allowed millions to move into occupations superior in reward to those of their parents, and even into the highest ranks of government and Party. And communist ideology, which celebrates internationalism and eschews discrimination, not only of class, but also of gender or colour, has evoked powerful responses both within and outside communist countries and has also been a reality in formerly colonial territories from Central Asia to Cuba and China.

At the top levels, in Eastern Europe at least, the privileges of the ruling elites have, however, long become sharply inconsistent with the ideology of equality. They include access to special shops, imported goods, trips abroad, private cars, country homes, subsidized holidays, tickets to the opera, and so forth. In the aftermath of the breakaway by Yugoslavia from the Soviet bloc in 1948, Milovan Djilas, a leading communist theoretician and political figure, revived the kind of ideas we saw foreshadowed above by the Italian elite theorists and by theorists like James Burnham and Adolf Berle who argued that ownership and control had become separated in the large capitalist corporation. This kind of argument may not be very convincing in relation to Ford or ICI, but is more illuminating than conventional Marxist class theory when applied to communist industry and government. In *The New Class* (1957) Djilas argued that in communist countries, including Yugoslavia, the Party, by virtue of its control over the political machinery, had brought into being a new form of society where the basis of the power of the ruling class was not *economic*: private ownership of the means of production: but monopoly of *political* authority. It was political power over public institutions, not private economic power, that gave this truly 'ruling' class control over the economy, and thereby access to economic privileges, rather than — as in Marx's model of capitalism — economic power (the 'base') manifesting itself in political terms (the State being simply a 'committee of the whole bourgeoisie'). Not surprisingly, Djilas was imprisoned for writing the book.

Citizens of Eastern European countries are fully aware of the existence of this economically privileged political class and of the wealthy managerial and professional elites. But many of them hope to become part of these classes themselves, or at least that their children or relatives might. Moreover, they are so severely circumscribed in terms of political self-expression that they are often resigned, cynical, or simply, pragmatically, 'work the system' in whatever way benefits them most, whilst conforming where they have to and keeping out of trouble. They have also experienced significant improvements in living standards, even including the now-reduced peasantry, who at last have access to welfare services like health and education, along with city folk, for the first time. Even Soviet refugees interviewed abroad therefore express strong support for state ownership of industry and regard the health, welfare and educational services and the absence of either unemployment or boom and slump with approval. The features most disliked by sectional interest groups (apart from ethnic discrimination, e.g. on the part of the Jews) were the collective farms, by the peasants, since low earnings are only made tolerable by complementary earnings from private plots (which provide much of the key foodstuffs on only 3% of the cultivated land), and on the part of the intelligentsia, a loathing of enforced ideological conformity.

But pride in the Soviet Union is also real. The isolation of the inter-War period, followed by the breakthrough to industrialization and the solidarity induced by the defeat of the Nazi invasion, the end of mass terror, and the easing of total social control have resulted in a very strong nationalism. Finally, the extent to which communist ideology — usually considered in the outside world to be boring, and cynically ignored by Soviet citizens — has really become internalized in the minds of those exposed to little else, is vastly underestimated in the West, which gives undue prominence to what are, in reality, a small handful of largely intellectual dissidents (however justified or significant these latter might be).

National varieties of socialism become inevitable the moment that socialism began to be constructed within a single nation-state. After the expected world revolution failed to occur in 1914, communist parties switched to a policy of fighting to achieve socialism within the boundaries of their respective bourgeois states, which many socialists had long advocated anyhow. They retained internationalism as a principle, and it remains a powerful one, as Cuban intervention to defend the Angolan revolution against South African repression has shown recently. But in the inter-war epoch, in practice, since there was only one 'socialist' society, internationalism at that time came to mean defence of the Soviet Union. Yet the logic of 'socialism in one country' was bound, eventually, to result in conflicts between socialist states and even within the Soviet Union once socialism became established in several nation-states.

Under Lenin, foreign communist parties had to subscribe to no fewer than twenty-one conditions, one of them being 'ready to give all possible' aid to the Soviet republics in their struggle against counter-revolution before they could be acknowledged as proper communist parties by being allowed to affiliate to the new Communist International.

The collapse of an internationalist strategy and ideology in 1914 had presented new problems, but also new positive possibilities for communist parties. The struggle for social justice promised by communism could continue. But it could now be combined with the hope of *national* liberation from foreign capitalist control, a policy which could appeal to a very much wider range of classes, especially in countries severely dominated and exploited by the imperialist West, than could any call to merely proletarian revolution. In China, the communists, wiped out in the cities, took to the countryside, where nine out of ten of the population lived. Virtually without resources, they had to develop support by defending the interests of the people they lived amongst, and thereby building up support: distributing land, building schools and bridges, providing rudimentary health services, and, above all, defending the people from Japanese fascist attack and despoliation and encouraging them to stand up for themselves.

But there were serious costs entailed in the emergence of communist nationalism, as Trotsky had emphasized. With the rise of numerous 'socialisms in one country'; in the absence of any serious machinery for a planned *inter*national socialist economy, COMECON apart; and by emphasizing the maximization of production rather than equalizing income as between richer and poorer zones and countries, socialist countries today actually compete with each other both on the world market and for economic advantages within the Second World. Nor is their nationalism merely an economic nationalism. They have developed a strong political identity, too, especially those countries that underwent years, sometimes decades, of revolutionary war. The two greatest socialist Powers, Russia and China, have ended up at each other's throats, and what nineteenth-century socialists would have believed impossible has actually occurred: war between socialist countries, notably Vietnam, China and Kampuchea.

The major rival to Soviet communism, Chinese communism, developed virtually independently of Soviet control or assistance, having established control of a sizeable piece of North-west China, in Yenan, where it developed the military guerrilla tactics that brought it to power in 1949, basing itself on the peasantry rather than the working class. The Chinese communists were also able to use the experience of the USSR as both a positive and a negative model. They thus introduced the 'democratic-centralist' model of Party organization and the Party-Government relationship, Soviet forms of economic planning and massive mobilization, and eventually, in 1958, some aspects of the Soviet agricultural system: the organization of agriculture and of rural life in general within large-scale communes in which the system of reward was based on work-points. But they avoided the major disasters of Russian policy: over-centralization; the exploitation of the peasantry in the interests of the city population; unqualified priority to heavy industry; and rapid, enforced collectivization in agriculture. Instead, lacking capital but rich in labour-power, and seeking to avoid resort to compulsion — in the extreme, terror — they used the machinery of persuasion ('ideological remoulding') to mobilize the population for long-term development. Though this has not yet resulted in any very dramatic material improvements by Western standards, at the very least it has ended the famines and malnutrition which were endemic in pre-communist semi-colonial China and laid the foundations for an industrial 'take-off'.

Communism has thus 'paid-off' materially, if slowly. But 'material incentives' are always accompanied by intensive appeals to altruistic labour for the common good, which the Chinese call 'moral incentives'. A similar emphasis can be found in the speeches of Che Guevara in Cuba before he went to his death fighting as a guerrilla in Bolivia. The balance between material incentives and moral appeals is always ambiguous and always shifting. Inequalities had certainly become serious in China by 1965 — a 'New Class' had emerged and was consolidating itself. The volcanic outbreak of the Cultural Revolution of 1966 expressed the resentments of young (and therefore low-paid) people against those who were better-off, attracting them to join in bitter revolutionary denunciations of the privileged. And even the recent extension of bonus incentives and encouragement of production on the tiny private plots still leaves China a vastly more egalitarian — and poorer — country than the USSR. The communes, in which eight out of ten of the population live, were established only after cooperatives had gradually replaced small-scale individual peasant agriculture, and they have more autonomy and have provided a more direct and appreciable return for both individual and collective effort than did the brutally-imposed collective farms in the USSR. Living standards have risen slowly, and with hiccups, but, over-all, steadily, so that appeals both to hard work and to social conscience ('political consciousness') do not solely meet with cynical responses.

Communism has therefore 'paid off' in recent decades, whether in

Eastern Europe, in China, or in newer communist countries like Vietnam which was able to defeat Japanese, French and United States imperialism successively only by virtue of communist leadership. It has also paid off even in the advanced capitalist countries, where communists, whether numerous, as in Italy, or few, are well-organized and have consistently been prominent as dedicated individuals, and through their contribution to trade union and other organizations in which they work incessantly to defend their fellow-workers — as in the Italian cities and the Indian states where they have been elected to power and where their administration is noted for its honesty and efficiency. It is for this reason, and not — as 'conspiracy theory' would have it — because they deceive people as to their true intentions or manipulate ill-attended trade union meetings, that they have been so strongly represented in trade union leaderships in so many Western countries, out of all proportion to the numbers of actual communists. Yet, Italy apart, they have been quite unable to convert this industrial support into votes, since though workers are quite happy to have communists win higher wages for them, they are not prepared to have secret police in Pittsburgh or Gulags in Scotland. The exceptional case is Italy, where the communists are the main mass opposition party. The reason for this is that their programme is in fact an extremely mild 'reformist' policy, little distinguishable from that of the social-democratic parties of other Western countries such as Britain's Labour Party, or that of Sweden, where the Social Democrats were in power with only one interruption from 1932 to 1976 but simply operated a welfare capitalism, with strong emphasis upon the 'corporate' representation of labour in industry and government.

If communism has 'paid off', then so has capitalism. The crucial differences between capitalism after 1945 and pre-war capitalism have been, firstly, the expansion of the economy, and secondly, the 'safety net' provided for the underprivileged by welfare services. Plainly, welfare provision, even if it continues to provide insurance against actual hunger, does nothing to cope with the structural problems of capitalism that underlie the present worldwide recession and the resulting mass unemployment, chronic inflation and declining growth rates. Yet even Eastern Europeans are fully aware of the continuing superiority of Western capitalism in providing, hitherto, higher levels of individual consumption for the great majority of the population, even though poverty is still endemic in the West among large stigmatized categories like women, immigrants, and other ethnic minorities. The advanced capitalist countries have, however, been able to prevent this disprivilege turning into serious discontent without needing to resort to forcible repression, not merely because extremes of poverty have been mitigated through welfare systems, but because they have further been able to 'engineer' and maintain consent via a skilful control of the media of mass communication which, although overwhelmingly strongly in favour of capitalism, present themselves as open to public opinion, or, in a few cases (like the BBC), are not even privately-owned at all. The majority of people, too, firmly believe in the system of parliamentary democracy and of the moral right of the party winning most votes to rule, even when they do not support the winning party or its policies. They also remain unenthusiastic about socialism, since they see the communist countries as a military threat to themselves, and as countries in which the mass of the people have lower living standards than in the West, whilst having nothing like the same freedom of expression. Paradoxically, military competition with the capitalist world forces the communist bloc into an economically disastrous competitive arms race in which the capitalist world has kept the lead and caused the communist countries to give defence priority over consumption.

But the problems of Soviet society are not simply problems caused by such external pressures. Marxist theoreticians in the Soviet Union generally claim that the contradiction of class society caused by private ownership of the means of production have been eliminated. Nevertheless they recognize that social classes still exist: there is said to be a working class, a peasantry, and an 'intelligentsia' that covers just about everything else — from managers to intellectuals, politicians and professionals. Thus these contradictions are acknowledged as still remaining in Soviet society, and not until the 'second stage' of communism proper will classes disappear. But, they say — and in contrast to capitalist society — such contradictions are not 'antagonistic' — there is no fundamental opposition of interests and therefore no class struggle between one class and another. Further socialist planning is said to harmonize and balance out what inequalities and conflicts there are. Far more adequate an explanation of the absence of overt industrial unrest is, simply, that it is not permitted. As a result, when life becomes *too* intolerable, the only way to express protest is by violent rioting, such as has occurred from East Germany in 1953 to the present day, and has at times sparked off political protests which, at their worst, have resulted in Soviet invasion to restore order, as in Hungary in 1956 or Czechoslovakia in 1968. For the first time in the history of the Leninist states of Eastern Europe, in Poland at least the possibility of the direct expression of the workers' interests, independent of Party control, seems to be growing.

Chinese theorists likewise claim to have a society characterized by 'non-antagonistic contradictions'. Yet Mao Tse-Tung went very much further than any other communist-state theorist in listing a whole series of contradictions still persisting in Chinese society — not only the 'Three Great Differences', but also contradictions between the State and the factories and communes, between the Party and people not in the Party, between the Han ('Chinese') majority people and the national minorities, and even 'between right and wrong'!

In the 'peripheral' capitalist countries of the Third World, force and blatant manipulation play a much more important role than they do in 'the West'. The response, in consequence, has often been radical and even revolutionary, rather than reformist and peaceable. Such countries, being underdeveloped producers of raw materials and foodstuffs, have hitherto been predominantly agrarian countries; their revolutions have therefore inevitably been peasant revolutions, despite Marx's assumption that the contradictions of capitalism would come to a head in the most developed capitalist countries. At the end of their lives, he and Engels both became much more aware that the revolution, which naturally had to be based on the 'immense majority' of the population, would necessitate mobilizing peasants as well as workers in the less-developed countries even though this recognition in fact called for major revision of their model of capitalist world development — a revision which they never undertook. Marx's overly economistic model also neglected both the capacity of the ruling class in developed capitalist societies to use the State to overcome economic problems by measures of redistribution ranging from 'progressive' taxation to welfare payments, and the importance of strategies of 'cultural hegemony', including nationalism, that would lead to the vertical incorporation of the working class.

But Marx was right in seeing capitalism as an increasingly urban and industrial form of society, for millions of people have flocked to the urban areas in the last decade, and within our lifetime an actual majority of the world's population will live in towns and cities. Whether there will be work for them is the single most important threat to the future continuation of capitalism — apart from the possibility of mutual nuclear annihilation. Yet despite this urban growth, there are twice as many people in the world's countryside as there were in 1900, and their conditions of life are inferior, for the most part, to those even of the urban poor. Seeking a better life for themselves, migration to the city offers an individualistic way out. But where no such personal alternatives seem possible either in the village or in the town, peasants have turned to collective solutions: in the extreme, to revolution. In the 1960s, Marxists devoted much argument, and some blood, to wrestling over the questions as to whether the proletariat was still the main agency of revolution or the peasantry. Some argued that the latter, being even more exploited and more numerous, would replace the proletariat as the motor of the historical change. Lenin, in *Imperialism*, had argued that a small privileged stratum among the working class had emerged in the imperialistic countries, and had been 'bought off'. This had been possible because other workers, in the colonies, had been exploited even more intensively. The existence of a 'labour aristocracy' of this kind did not come about only with the advent of imperialism, however, for ruling classes have always manipulated privileged minorities amongst the working people in order to 'divide and rule' and enlisted people who were of humble origins to work at keeping down those who criticized their rule.

But the 'labour aristocracy' rapidly grew into a sizeable population, not a mere handful, and the gap between the proletariats of the 'centre' and workers and peasants in the 'peripheral', dependent capitalist countries who were exploited far more ruthlessly — between 'North' and 'South' — grew ever greater. By the 1960s, Frantz Fanon, a major theorist of Third World revolution, had extended Lenin's argument by asserting that the *whole* population of the Western world, not just the upper and middle classes, and not just a small segment of the working class either, were living off the sweat of the Third World. The working class had consequently become corrupted and no longer had revolutionary potential. Even within Third World countries themselves, he argued, the working class were privileged, with better pay and better conditions, at work and outside it, than the rural poor. Hence the revolution would be a peasant revolution, assisted, in the towns, not by the proletariat, but by the new immigrant population unable to find work (for which he used the unfortunate label 'lumpenproletariat'), and a section of the new intelligentsia.

He clearly exaggerated the prosperity of the majority of the working class in most underdeveloped countries, and ignored, in any case, their rising expectations, which most sociologists regard as a greater potential stimulus to revolution than the persistence of traditional poverty. But he was right to emphasize that, so far, communist and nationalist revolutions have only been made in overwhelmingly peasant countries. Despite this, Marxist leaderships have retained the label 'proletarian' to describe these movements, even when 95% of their guerrilla armies have been of peasant origin — on the grounds that the revolution began in the cities, or that its programme had historically emerged out of the capitalism Marx had analysed and out of the response of the working class to that exploitation. They have been reluctant, that is, to abandon the dogma that the proletariat is *the* revolutionary force, even when proletariats have been either non-existent or relatively unimportant. Given persisting misery in both town and countryside, it is likely that there will also be persisting opposition to that misery, both amongst peasants, ex-peasants now constituting a new and sizeable 'urban poor', and even among the only marginally better-off working classes held down by force in the interest of classes who appropriate a far higher share of national income than even their counterparts in the USA, Western Europe, or Japan. The security of these exploited classes is also further threatened now by the economic crisis gripping the entire capitalist world, which is bound to affect them much worse than their counterparts in the First World.

Even during the twenty years of overall capitalist growth following World War II, communist revolutions have continued to occur — in Cuba and Vietnam — and Marxist-led movements have come to power in Angola, Mozambique, Nicaragua and Afghanistan. Overall, however, capitalism has been able to maintain itself in the heartlands, and even in the largest very poor countries such as India, Pakistan, Indonesia or Bangladesh either because they have still been able to command majority popular support, or because, where this has been lacking, governments have simply depended upon repression, backed by the capacity of the advanced capitalist countries, especially the USA, to provide the means of military and other repression.

Resort to force and resort to the manipulation of consent vary inversely: regimes which are low in popularity have to resort the more to violence. But in estimating the viability of capitalism, or of any other political system, we need a more sophisticated model than one which possesses only these two variables. Capitalism persists because its economic efficiency enables it to pay off, not only for the upper and middle classes, but for at least enough of the producing and exploited classes, at the lowest level sufficiently to ensure at least survival, and in richer countries, much more than mere survival. The capacity to 'buy off', and the size of the population thus privileged, obviously varies with the productive power of the economy. They also depend upon political and not merely economic variables: the flexibility, decisiveness, cohesiveness and organization of the ruling class and likewise of the working and other classes they exploit and rule. In this political equation, cultural hegemony — the capacity to persuade the ruled and exploited of the justice or inevitability of these arrangements — is usually a major independent variable.

Revolution is unlikely to occur in the absence of collapse on all these fronts simultaneously: when the means of violence becomes unreliable — when the Army becomes disaffected, or the forces ranged against it too strong (as in the Shah's Iran); when the regime can no longer command the natural loyalty of even all of the wealthier classes, and has forfeited popular loyalty altogether; when the economy can no longer meet the expectations of the masses; when the masses feel that the traditional political institutions get them nowhere; when the ruling class loses its nerve and resorts to brutality and massacre — or fails to act decisively; when the revolutionaries have developed an efficient machinery of their own; and when economic recession no longer permits concessions to be made to the masses except at the expense of the power and wealth of the ruling classes. Lenin, who knew a good deal about revolutions, expressed all this pithily in his observation that revolutions occurred "not just when the 'exploited' and oppressed masses understand the impossibility of living in the old way and demand changes but when the exploiting classes are also no longer able to live and rule in the old way".

Plainly, capitalism in its imperialist heartlands is a very long way yet from any such generalized collapse. Yet its popularity has always been ambiguous and qualified and still is. Work has become increasingly alienating, not less so, for more and more millions in industry who have become 'appendages of machines' in ways that were inconceivable when that phrase was coined in the nineteenth century: when, on the automobile assembly line, the worker's movements are now timed in seconds where twenty-five years ago they were timed in minutes, and as non-manual jobs, too, have become increasingly routinized. Leaving aside capitalism's capacity to find work for everybody, work, for the great majority of those who do have it, has become increasingly merely a means to an end — a still lengthy, arduous, sometimes exhausting, dangerous and degrading, and nearly always boring necessity endured in order to make possible a meaningful non-work life in the home and in leisure-time pursuits. Resentment of the rich, and massive gaps in consumption, provide a permanent breeding-ground for discontent. Capitalism, then, remains vulnerable to the withdrawal of mass support and to serious dislocation even in its heartlands, as May 1968 showed in France and as the current, far more serious, world crisis shows. The contradictions of capitalism, then, have proved to be far from some mere figment of the fevered imagination of left-wingers fixated upon having a revolution. Nor can they be as easily readily controlled or eliminated as was assumed to be the case during the long Keynesian post-war period. Keynesian theories and remedies disappeared virtually without trace after 1974. But unemployment under modern capitalism, in the 'centre' at least, still does not mean starvation, whatever frustration and indignity it may bring.

The 'point of production' beloved of economistic Marxists is by no means the only focus of discontent, however, nor the only denial of humanity under capitalism. Whole categories of humankind are still stigmatized and exploited because of their (quite non-economic) attributes, notably sex and colour. The survival of human beings of any class or category becomes increasingly problematic with the steady escalation of the nuclear balance of terror and as the earth's resources are despoiled in the name of ever-increasing consumption, especially on the part of the USA, which consumes around a third of the world's output of many major commodities. And because of the unplanned nature of the market, even in the epoch of giant 'multinational' corporations, earlier Marxist criticism of the 'anarchic' nature of capitalism seems mild in a world poisoned by pollution and obsessed by consumerism and 'planned obsolescence', but where hundreds of millions go hungry though the technical capacity to feed them does exist.

Work in communist countries is similarly unrewarding, only mitigated to the extent that improvements in output get passed on to the producers, and to the extent that participation in decision-making exists, usually at lower levels, as in the Chinese communes or the Yugoslav 'self-managed' enterprises. Given the nature of the political system in those countries, opposition over this issue or that, if it grows into something serious, tends to result in opposition to the state, and thereby to become 'political'. But because of the immense power in the hands of those who control the political apparatuses, opposition is exceptionally difficult, and since there are few effective legitimate channels for expressing criticism of public policy the most effective forms of protest have been illegitimate and unconstitutional, such as riots and strikes, which easily escalate into violence even though they may only be aimed at achieving quite limited demands.

But the alternatives, in either system, are not breakdown or repression. There are innumerable intermediate possibilities, and neither capitalism nor communism shows any likelihood of collapse in the visible future. One way that capitalism has historically been able to avoid social breakdown has been to innovate economically and technologically, and thereby refute the notion of 'limits to growth'. By introducing microchips, robots, the exploitation of the resources of outer space, biological engineering, and the development of new ways of harnessing energy, higher production and productivity could be achieved, with resulting (unequal) distribution of the enlarged product. Communist countries likewise rely on the expansion of the forces of production to solve their social problems.

Marx believed that authentic socialism would emerge in economically advanced countries, which had developed the economic resources which could make better material living standards possible for all, and where political rights had been won, organization perfected, and consciousness matured among the working class. In such societies, a working class coming to power would not be faced with having to institute ruthless control in order to mobilize the people for modernization, for they would be taking over already developed economies. They would also have a richer tradition of popular participation in the running of the whole gamut of social institutions at every level, including a highly diversified range of popular organizations — parties, trade unions, voluntary associations, and local government organs. Nor are these hard-won rights and now well-established institutions easily given up. Further, criticism and opposition are ingrained and regarded not as crimes, but as civic rights and duties. The likelihood of copying authoritarian models borrowed from the communisms of backward countries and repeating their disasters can be avoided. Whether ruling classes would accept defeat without resorting to a massive application of centralized force in a total showdown which would eliminate those freedoms altogether and provoke authoritarian responses on the Left is unpredictable.

And there is a further scenario that Marx never envisaged: that capitalism and communism — or one of their component countries or movements — could pull down the whole temple, by provoking nuclear war, rather than allow the frustration of their private interests.

Such a holocaust might well not result from any direct confrontation between the leading capitalist or communist countries, initially at any rate, but from quite other persisting cultural and historical antagonisms, such as Zionism, the new Muslim challenges to the West, or the innumerable smaller nationalist resentments. But they would inevitably feed into, and therefore spark off, the confrontation between the Superpowers that Mao called the 'principle contradiction'. His own indomitable optimism — since he believed that evolution would start all over again after such an Armageddon — has not convinced many people as being realistic.

Marxism, Sociology and Utopia

In Praise of Communism

It's quite straightforward, you'll understand it. It's not hard.
Because you're not an exploiter, you'll quite easily grasp it.
It's for your own good, so find out all about it.
They're fools who describe it as foolish, and foul who describe it
　　as foulness.
It's against all that's foul and against all that's foulness.
The exploiters will tell you it's criminal
But we know better:
It puts an end to all that's criminal.
It isn't madness, but puts
An end to all madness.
It doesn't mean chaos
It just means order.
It's just the simple thing
That's hard, so hard to do.

by Bertolt Brecht

In one sense, this book has been devoted to showing that communism is not only 'hard to do', but also, as theory, nothing like as 'simple' as Brecht claimed. Were it so straightforward, there would not only be no need for the mounting pile of interpretations of Marx: they would not even be possible. Nor would the bitter disputes be fought out sometimes with guns rather than words.

But the ambiguities are there, as well as the plain failure of much that has happened since Marx's day to happen in the way that his theory suggested. Gramsci and Mao — both practitioners of revolutionary politics — emphasized that Marxism was not a positivistic, detached theory: it was a 'guide to action'. The inability of Marx to predict the future did not really damage Marxism at all, Gramsci argued, for it was not some kind of crystal-ball gazing that told you what would happen, independently of human will, as it were. Rather, Marxism was a body of theory that told you what was worth striving for, and which provided general outlines as to how to carry forward that struggle. It identified the enemy, told you who your allies were, showed you your own place in society, indicated the general line of march, and pointed out the main agencies of change and of resistance to change. "One 'foresees'", Gramsci wrote, "to the extent to which one acts, to which one makes a voluntary effort and so contributes concretely to creating the 'foreseen' result".

Gramsci's Marxism thus falls into the category I have labelled 'Promethean': the Marxism that seeks to change the world, as distinct from the 'system Marxisms' that seek to order and organize it, both intellectually and practically. Gouldner has seized upon a similar distinction in his classification of the varieties of Marxisms into 'Critical' Marxism and 'Scientific' Marxism respectively. Naturally, it is the latter that appeals to governments and leaderships. It has been argued that to understand the course of Soviet history you need to use a critical kind of Marxism for the revolutionary period, but that functionalism is more useful for an understanding of the operations of the consolidated and rigidly-integrated post-revolutionary Soviet state. Alternatively, one can see official Soviet Marxism as precisely an alternative, functionalist form of Marxism.

Mao-Tse Tung, now denigrated by his enemies as a mere homespun peasant philosopher, also argued that Marxism was a way of distinguishing the important causal factors in history from the unimportant, the causal from the caused: it enabled you, above all, to seize the 'principal contradiction'. For these revolutionaries, Marxism was thus no mere theoretical scheme, or a tool for running an established social order, but a means of constantly challenging the routinization of power.

Above all, it answered Lenin's revolutionary question 'What is to be *Done*?'

György Lukács, a leading figure in a failed revolution, in Hungary, not only reverted to an idealistic version of Marxism, but produced the extreme claim that it would not matter if every one of Marx's particular propositions were to be proved false, since Marxism was not a bundle of prophecies, but a general methodology, an ingenious distortion which only a philosopher could produce, since most people would reasonably assume that if all the conclusions a particular methodology led to proved to be untrue, there must be something fundamentally wrong with the basic methodology.

Of course, you can have a marvellous, and even correct, analysis, and the other person has all the guns. But there is more to Marxism's difficulties than that. Most Marxists refuse to admit, or even to envisage, that basic Marxist principles can be applied to Marxism; above all, that Marxism itself might contain contradictions built into the theoretical system as such. At worst, they display a blind unwillingness to question the received ideas they repeat. This is not revolutionary thinking, however revolutionary such people might be in their political practice. But in their intellectual activity, they are conservative and uncritical. Without getting side-tracked into a linguistic/philosophical discussion as to what constitutes a 'contradiction', or a 'fundamental' contradiction, intrinsic to Marxism is the dynamic tension between the subjective and the objective: the central dialectic: in its simplest and most extreme terms, between ideas and the social arrangements within which we lead our lives.

It is my contention that the model of base and superstructure which most Marxists, including Marx, took as the key image through which to express the essence of their theoretical system, is in fact quite incompatible with the idea of a *dialectical* science of society, since it implies not only conceptually isolating the economy in an unacceptable way, but also assumes that the latter somehow is necessarily more decisive than anything else. It therefore leads, inexorably, to one of two temptations: the more normal temptation of materialist 'reductionism': the belief that the so-called base can be separated from the so-called superstructure (which it can't); that the base is 'material' (which it isn't); and that it determines the rest (which it doesn't). Politically, it leads to several delusions for instance, the notion that the important thing is to act, and that theory will somehow come out alright in the process of acting. The other temptation is rarer amongst ordinary people, but typical of intellectuals: the assumption that the clarification of theory takes precedence over everything else.

There can never be an end to these theoretical debates and practical political delusions and oscillations as long as the 'base/superstructure' model is retained, for the model itself, being unsatisfactory, constantly requires repair jobs of the kind we have noted from Engels to the present day.

The second crucial contradiction in most varieties of Marxism is a temptation shared with other systematic sociologies and indeed scientific frameworks in general: the 'holistic' temptation to over-connect everything, for instance, to treat the family as an 'ideological State apparatus'. Such Marxisms are over-systematic, over-deterministic, and over-economistic. Over-systematic, because they do not allow, as Gouldner has argued in the case of another overly systematic sociology, the functionalism of Talcott Parsons, enough 'relative autonomy' to the component parts of the social system. By concentrating on the integration of the entire social order at a given point in time — 'syn-chronically' — they neglect the historical dimension: how institutions persist over centuries and epochs, and become successively adapted, though not necessarily in every respect, even though new modes of production become dominant. Yet, as Perry Anderson has shown, the history of Western capitalist society cannot be comprehended without an understanding of the legacy not only of the previous feudal epoch, but even the heritage of Greece and Rome and the institutions trans-mitted through the centuries via the Roman Catholic Church. For any particular country, the way all these elements will be combined will necessarily be different, and can certainly not be reduced to some simple scheme of the 'articulation of modes of production', since it involves the whole of the cultural order over long periods of historical time, and, too, relations with other societies and cultural communities. Marxism, institutionalised as communism, is itself the basis of a supra-societal cultural community, since it retains the notion of 'proletarian inter-nationalism', and assists revolutionary movements despite the con-comitant emergence of communist nation-states.

Finally, most Marxisms are over-deterministic in a way peculiar to Marxism, in that they isolate 'the economic' and then attribute to its causal predominance.

It is perfectly understandable why these distortions have come about: for the same reasons that they did in Marx's day, for Marxists have taken materialism as the essence of their world-view, in opposition to what they rightly see as predominantly idealist theories. Yet in so doing they have done precisely what Marx said he had no intention of doing (but what Weber said he *had* done): producing a 'one-sided' materialism in response to a one-sided idealism. Neither alternative begins to resemble what Marx said he was engaged in: producing a *dialectical* science of society.

Of course, the nettle has to be grasped: Marx didn't just say that everything influenced everything else, or that ideas might steer society to one degree, and economic necessity to another. He quite clearly emphasized the *necessity* of producing. He also put at the heart of his sociology — as no other sociology does — the theme of exploitation: that there is a constant struggle in which dominant minorities strive to monopolize socially-produced wealth, and a constant counter-claim for social justice. Most modern sociology now recognizes that classes, constituted by virtue of ownership or non-ownership of the means of production, are indeed crucial, but so too are all other, numerous forms of exploitation — of race, gender, ethnicity — which are based on status inequalities that get translated *into* economic inequalities. Proletarians have no monopoly of exploitation, and it is only under the conditions of the theoretically pure capitalist market that economic classes of that kind become predominant. In historical epochs before that, and in the underdeveloped capitalist world today, status-based inequalities are more widespread than pure class struggle. And we now see more clearly that even under regimes ideologically committed to socialist egalitarianism, the struggle goes on in new ways, this time in terms of politically-regulated access to privileges rather than the inequalities built into the logic of a market economy.

The necessity of production by no means determines who gets what. Even less is this determined by technological factors. Marx's theories were not, in his view, an 'economics'; they were political economy. But given the positivistic intellectual climate of his day, when Romanticism had been defeated by natural science, and because he lived before the epoch which saw not only the recovery of consciousness, but the further dramatic discovery of the unconscious, Marx was unable to create an adequate model of culture, through which the products of human consciousness have been accumulated over millennia and distilled, communicated, handed on, and added to in forms ranging from books to oral tradition.

Marxists have often tried to remedy these deficiencies by borrowing from 'bourgeois' social science, which had no inhibitions about exploring the non-material and therefore made important progress, particularly in the form of the major social science that emerged after Marx and Engels' deaths: psychology. In the shape of Freud's psychoanalytical theories, it opened up a Pandora's box of irrational forces hitherto locked up or unsuspected but now let loose to shock the orthodox, whilst also offering the possibility of bringing the individual into social theory, and of linking the understanding of the individual to the understanding of society – thereby rejecting what one sociologist, Dennis Wrong, has called an 'over-socialized conception of man', and in the words of another, George Homans, thereby 'bringing man back in'.

But though it inspired some imaginative thinking, notably the work of the Frankfurt School in pre-Hitler Germany, Freudian theory rested upon such debatable assumptions about human motivation and its sources, and about the relationship of these to social conditioning, that it could be fitted to the 'base/superstructure' model only by elaborate intellectual contortions, dubious analogies, or poetic imagery. This is not so serious, insofar as the latter model is invalid anyway. But it becomes more serious when the novel – and valuable – stress upon the instinctual and the irrational, and upon sexuality, become converted into pessimistic dogmas and thereby stand in the way of developing a truly social psychology in which the individual is indeed to be recognized as having pre-social drives. These may manifest themselves in ways society approves of or disapproves of – but a distinction still needs to be drawn between the social production of frustration, aggressive behaviour and the like – in individuals, in group life and between types of persons – and the idealist mystification that treats war, exploitation and criminality as if they were simply 'aggregate' manifestations of tensions which basically derive from the personalities of 'pre-social' individuals.

Marxism also distinguishes the *societal* from the social. Yet although societies do constitute wholes, their boundaries are never absolutely impermeable, and any society has relations with others which may be negative or positive and which exhibit varying degrees of systematic organization. Between the level of the society and the individual, too, stand intermediate levels and forms of social organization, of which Marxism selects social classes as the decisive ones. It does so at a cost: that of underestimating the importance of other social groupings, subcultures and levels of social organization of great immense importance, from ethnic categories to face-to-face groups. Until recently, Marxism has left the study of these, for the most part, to proponents of other approaches, to the great disadvantage of Marxism, which in consequence has seemed to be unilluminating to people who want to understand deviant behaviour, gender-differences, the family and its alternatives, or the nature of race prejudice.

Conversely, the idealistic treatment of these very areas reveals what has been lost by failing to use the insights that Marxism insists upon. To discuss, racial antagonism, for instance, as generations of psychologists have done, predominantly in terms of innate or culturally transmitted prejudices — of attitudes — is an idealist distortion which Marxism avoids. It is also a false starting-point. The 11 million migrant labourers in Western Europe; the Indians, Pakistanis, West Indians and Irish immigrants in Britain, do have to be seen as part of the functioning of capitalism, which sucks in cheap labour in times of expansion and tries to get rid of it in times of contraction. Further, resentment against such newcomers is not simply a 'natural' human propensity, some inherent dislike of strangers, as idealist theory would have it, but is fuelled by fear of economic competition for jobs, housing, and other social goods.

Marxism thus thrusts to the centre of the stage — and criticizes — this competition over resources which other theories tend to treat merely as something in the background which we can take as given and do not need to focus upon. Marxists have tended, too often, on the other hand, to always stress material interests, too narrowly: mainly in terms of wages and conditions of work-life, vital as these are, neglecting other kinds of relations outside work — in the neighbourhood, in churches, in recreation, etc. — which may indeed be connected with one's work-role, but not in any simple way. Voting behaviour, religious affiliation, or the way we spend our leisure time, are demonstrably class-related to a significant extent, but the relationship is by no means a neat fit, and usually takes the form of a statement of probability. Further, the connections between social institutions and ideas which exist at one point in time do not necessarily persist: ideas about the virtue of charity or of hard work are shared today by people who are no longer Christians. Hence at a general theoretical level, Marxists would do well to replace their language of determination of the non-economic by the economic by a more flexible concept, invented by a political enemy of Marx, but whose greatest tribute to the power of the latter's thought was to spend his life, it has been said, in a debate with Marx's ghost. Max Weber argued that there was indeed an 'affinity' between the economic and the non-economic, between Protestantism and capitalism, but that the new capitalist economy of Reformation Europe did not *produce* Luther's ideas about consubstantiation, and tried instead to demonstrate the complex links between religious beliefs and new methods of producing iron or exploiting the labour of factory workers.

Other sociologies have filled the gaps and made the links Marxism has neglected or treated too crudely. Symbolic interactionism has taken the primary face-to-face, localized, interacting group as its starting-point, sometimes as if it were the only real constituent of everyday life.

For Herbert Blumer, for instance, Marx's classes were not real at all, but merely intellectual abstractions or categories which never acted together. It was people who did.

Hence, instead of 'reducing human society to social units that do not act — for example, social classes . . .', he argued, we should recognize that 'the individuals who composed human society . . . do not act toward culture, social structure or the like; they act toward situations'.

Other sociologies depart even more fundamentally from that of Marx, notably those idealistic theories which assert that the whole emphasis upon social structures is mistaken, because structures only work to the extent that people subscribe to rules, and it is these cultural codes that we ought to concentrate on since they bind society together or fail to.

After the recital above of the shortcomings of Marxism it might seem that, in the end, it has little to offer. Its power, however, is best seen by looking at its rivals, particularly when idealism degenerates into an apology for conservatism, by postulating consensus, common interests and shared cultural values or appeals to customary norms when we all know that these are the traditional appeals of those who want to play down the use of force, manipulation, and deceit and damp down social protest. By contrast, Marxism exposes precisely what such ideologies seek to conceal: their acceptance or justification of systems of *exploitation* which deprive the producers of the fruits of their labour. If material *interest* is thus central to Marxism, so are the concepts of immaterial *mystification* and of *false consciousness*, and the belief that human reason can be collectively applied to construct a society free from the conflicts built into all class systems.

Small group sociologies, by contrast, for all the light they have thrown on the internal dynamics of the milieux in which we spend most of our waking life, are usually devoid of any model of societies as wholes. The structure of society is taken as 'given' and somehow assumed to be known — or irrelevant. As C. Wright Mills put it, these are 'middle-level' images of society produced by people whose occupations are typically middle-level, but who lack the intellectual imagination to transcend their personal position, since that would require them to grasp, and formulate, a theory of society at national and supranational levels, and only then to situate their small groups within such a framework.

Conversely, Marxism's failure to develop a social psychology means that it has to borrow from those who *have* pioneered the study of interpersonal relations and of the way in which the Self is socially constructed: researches which have put into practice Marx's conception of the 'human essence' as the 'ensemble' of social relations, both for groups and categories and for individuals: an implicit but undeveloped project for a Marxist psychology which is quite incompatible with those travesties of Marx's thought that reduces humanity to *Homo economicus*, or which tries to develop a psychology by borrowing from non-sociological theories from Freud to behaviourism.

The second positive and valuable and fundamental aspect of symbolic interactionism has been the theoretical attention it has given to the other term in that phrase: symbols. Similarly, the emphasis in Weber upon the values which inform all action is another powerful contribution to the exploration of the subjective neglected by economistic Marxism.

In the end, Marxism is more than simply a cognitive scheme, a purely intellectual theory. That it is a guide to action is obvious. That it embodies a view of human nature — an ontology — and contains too, a vision of human potential — and therefore a system of moral values — is less often emphasized by its friends and its enemies, and by those who see it merely as an 'economic theory of history' or a purely scientific theory. For it contains a vision, not just of the destruction of capitalism, but of the ending of that long stretch of human history in which the exploitation of the many has been possible because the few have monopolized the means of production. It involves, therefore, a counter-culture: an alternative vision which seeks to replace competition by cooperation; private property by social ownership; individualism by comradeship; and possessiveness and acquisitiveness by altruism.

Such a vision is the reason for the constant regeneration of the appeal of Marxism despite its shortcomings and failings, especially among that half of humanity, the young, for whom the inhumanities of the Stalin era are something they only know about from books or from their parents. For them rather, the brutalities of a social order that condemns them to endemic hunger or a meaningless existence, and deprives them of access to the cultural riches of the world, are much more pressing problems than the negative face of communism which their rulers constantly remind them of.

Today, fewer people believe that socialism would be some kind of utopia. We have seen too much to believe that. But we do know that at the very least, starvation, poverty and brutal injustice visited by the powerful upon the weak are man-made, not acts of God, and can be eliminated — and that very much more might be achieved.

Marxism, for Marx, always entailed much more than minimal freedoms from hunger, exploitation, and unemployment. Humanity would only become truly human, Marx declared, when it moved 'beyond the sphere of actual material production'. He envisaged socialism as a form of society which would not only be economically superior to bourgeois society but also morally, because it would add to the formal equality of bourgeois society material equality and thereby introduce true freedom. These ideas have remained in abeyance or have sometimes been brutally suppressed in societies where Marxism has been an ideology mobilizing people for development. Until communism does increase freedoms across the board, rather than restrict them in the name of material improvement, and as long as new forms of privilege and power emerge, the fear will always remain, for the poor, that they might become better-off economically under communism, but politically and spiritually will simply be controlled in new ways. For the mass of the people in the richer Western world, there will seem little to gain economically either.

The appeal of Marxism, or of its hitherto institutionalized form, communism, is not, however, basically another religious ideology, analogous to Christian or Muslim dreams of heaven. Along with all atheism, Marxism posits that there is no meaning in the world, no good or bad, other than that created by human beings and relevant to human society, no forces controlling us from outside society. Of course, to argue and believe that social justice is a good thing is itself a value. Elitists regard the idea as mere romanticism; cynics believe that no society will ever be seriously just, so that ideas and ideals aiming at a more rational and harmonious social order might as well be junked and the race allowed to go to the strongest. The major philosophy opposed to such views, in today's world, is Marxism.

Suggestions for Further Reading

It is best to begin by reading the original writings of Marx and Engels before turning to later Marxists and to commentaries. When they finally appear, the collected writings of Marx and Engels will run to more than fifty volumes. The most important are probably these:

Marx: *Economic and Political Manuscripts of 1844*.
Marx: *Theses on Feuerbach* (1845).
Engels: *The Condition of the Working Class in England in 1844* (1845).
Marx: *Wage Labour and Capital* (1847).
Marx and Engels: *The Manifesto of the Communist Party* (1848).
Marx: *The Eighteenth Brumaire of Louis Bonaparte* (1852).
Marx: The Preface to *A Contribution to the Critique of Political Economy* (1859).
Marx: *Wages, Price and Profit* (1865).
Marx: *The Civil War in France* (1871).
Marx: *Critique of the Gotha Programme* (1875).
Engels: *Anti-Dühring*: Herr Eugen Dühring's Revolution in Science (1878).

All the above are contained in Marx and Engels, *Selected Works*, Lawrence and Wishart, London. Marx and Engels, *Selected Correspon-*

dence, Foreign Language Publishing House, Moscow, is a vital companion volume, together with Marx and Engels *On Britain*. All three are inexpensive editions, and in addition:

Marx: *Class Struggles in France* (1848-1850).
Marx's Grundrisse (1857-1858), a selection by David McLellan, Paladin Books, 1973.
Marx: *Capital*, Volume I.

The standard English biography of Marx is David McLellan's *Karl Marx: his Life and Thought*, (Macmillan, 1973). The first volume of Yvonne Kapp's superb study of *Eleanor Marx* (Lawrence and Wishart, 1972), provides a fascinating account of the domestic life of Marx and Engels.

Michael Evans' *Karl Marx* (Allen and Unwin, 1975) is a sound, lucid and succinct analysis of Marx's political thought. Derek Sayer's *Marx's Method: ideology, science and critique in 'Capital'* (Harvester, 1979) provides a clear and accurate distillation of Marx's economic ideas. Shlomo Avineri's *The Social and Political Thought of Karl Marx* (Cambridge University Press, 1970) emphasizes the influence of German idealist philosophy on Marx's thinking. A classic of scholarship which is also eminently readable is Edmund Wilson's 1940 study of the forerunners of Marx and Engels and of Lenin and Trotsky, *To The Finland Station* (Doubleday Anchor Book A6).

Marxism after Marx is best represented by practitioners of revolution. The two volumes of Lenin's *Selected Works* (Foreign Languages Publishing House, Moscow) contain most of his key writings, notably 'What is to be Done?', 'Two Tactics of Social Democracy', 'Imperialism', 'What the Friends of the People Are', 'One Step Forward, Two Steps Back', 'The State and Revolution', and "'Left-wing' Communism, an Infantile Disorder". Trotsky's compelling *History of the Russian Revolution* (one volume edition, Doubleday Anchor Books, A170) and *The Revolution Betrayed* (originally 1937, many editions), provide a dynamic contrast to the now virtually unobtainable *Short Course on the History of the Communist Party* (Bolsheviks), the 'Bible' of international communism in the Stalin era, once printed in hundreds of millions of copies and in dozens of languages. *Mao Tse-Tung Unrehearsed: talks and letters 1956-71*, edited by Stuart Schram (Penguin, 1974) contains much off-the-record material which can be read alongside the official *Selected Works*, particularly Volume I, which contains his essay 'On the Analysis of Classes in Chinese Society' and the important and fascinating 'Report on the Peasant Situation in Hunan' (*Selected Works*, Vol. I, 1954, Peking). In addition, his short essay 'On Contradiction' in *Essential Works of Chinese Communism*, ed. Winberg Chai,

(Bantam, New York, 1969) should be read and compared with the talk 'On the Ten Great Relationships' in the Schram volume. Antonio Gramsci's *The Modern Prince and other writings* (Lawrence and Wishart, 1957) contains the most important passages from Gramsci's writings.

For a valuable survey of Marxism closer to home, see Perry Anderson's *Considerations on Western Marxism* (New Left Books, London, 1976). A major theoretical school strongly influenced by Marxism in the inter-War period, the Frankfurt School, is portrayed in Martin Jay's *The Dialectical Imagination* (Heinemann, 1973). Finally, Marxist scholarship at its best is represented by E. J. Hobsbawm's *The Age of Revolution 1798–1848* (Mentor Books, London, 1964), *The Age of Capital 1848–1875* (Weidenfeld and Nicolson, 1975) and *Industry and Empire* (Penguin, 1969), in Christopher Hill's *Reformation to Industrial Revolution* (Penguin, Harmondsworth, 1969), and in Perry Anderson's *Passages from Antiquity to Feudalism* and *Lineages of the Absolutist State* (New Left Books, 1974).

Index